Fragments of a Lost Childhood

Zahava Kohn
in conversation with
Ann Rosen

Introduction by Sir Martin Gilbert

Quill

in association with

THE
HOLOCAUST
CENTRE

Fragments of a Lost Childhood

Zahava Kohn in conversation with Ann Rosen

Published in Great Britain by
Quill Press in association with The Holocaust Centre
The Hub,
Haskell House,
152 West End Lane
London. NW6 1SD

© 2009 Zahava Kohn
Reprinted October 2013

British Library Catalogue in Publication Data
A catalogue record for this book is available from the British
Library

ISBN 978-0-9555009-3-0

Design and artwork, The Holocaust Centre
Printed and bound by Jellyfish Print Solutions, Swanmore

Cover Photograph: Zahava, aged two

CONTENTS

In loving memory of my parents,
Rosy and Sigmund Kanarek

INTRODUCTION

Martin Gilbert

Conversations between Zahava Kohn and Ann Rosen have resulted in a book that does great service to all those interested in the Holocaust and tells the story of Zahava's survival and that of her mother and father, Rosy and Sigmund Kanarek. It is a story that emerged from a suitcase: one that Rosy had managed to keep with her in Bergen-Belsen, and which remained unopened for more than 60 years after Zahava and her parents were liberated.

Zahava was born two and a half years after Hitler came to power in Germany. Her parents, who had left Germany for Holland after the advent of Nazism, had just emigrated to Palestine. Zahava was born a Palestinian Jewish subject of the British Mandate. This fact was to prove the family's salvation.

Life in Palestine was hard for the Kanareks, as for so many of the refugee immigrants from Europe. Rosy became ill and in April 1937 the family left Palestine, settling in Holland. Zahava's memories of those years are hazy. From the contents of her mother's suitcase, with the encouragement of Ann Rosen, and with her own inner courage, she has pieced together this remarkable book.

At the end of 1941, the Kanareks handed over their one-year-old baby boy, Jehudi, to the Dutch resistance. He was taken for safety to a Christian orphanage where some 45 Jewish children were being looked after. When, a year later, the orphanage was raided by the Gestapo, 43 of the children were taken away and later sent to their deaths in Auschwitz. Blond, blue-eyed Jehudi was one of the two children left behind: he was thought to be 'Aryan' and was spared. For the rest of the war he was looked after by a Dutch Christian woman, Nurse Stol – his rescuer.

In May 1943, ten months after the beginning of the deportation of Jews from Holland to Auschwitz, the SS came to the Kanarek apartment in Amsterdam. Father, mother and daughter were taken to Westerbork transit camp. The documents and letters in Rosy's suitcase give a sense of daily life in the camp.

Rosy and Sigmund Kanarek were fortunate that their daughter had been born in Palestine. Unlike them, she had British protection. Because they stayed together, the parents benefited from their daughter's unusual status. Of the more than 100,000 Jews who were sent, like the Kanareks, to Westerbork, most were sent to their deaths at Auschwitz and Sobibor.

The Kanareks were among those selected to be sent to Auschwitz. When they were already on the Westerbork platform, they were told that they should return to the camp. As a protected British Mandate child, Zahava and her parents were being spared deportation in case there were to be an exchange of British citizens then detained in Holland for German citizens then detained in Palestine. Several such exchanges actually took place.

After nine months in Westerbork, the Kanareks were officially informed that they were to be sent to another camp 'for the Palestine exchange'. That camp was Bergen-Belsen. There, thanks also to the young Zahava's British protection, they survived: in the 'star camp' where they did not have to wear concentration camp clothes, but a yellow star on their ordinary clothes.

There was constant fear, which Zahava, then eight years old, vividly recalls. "I was terrified of the dogs and the guns." All her father's teeth were knocked out. The cards and letters in Rosy's suitcase give details of life in the camp, of their illnesses, and of the efforts being made to help them.

In January 1945, the Kanareks were among several hundred Jews in Bergen-Belsen sent to an internment camp at Biberach, a German town near the Swiss border, for eventual exchange with Germans held by the Allies. Rosy's suitcase contains several letters sent to her there. Her letters from Biberach also survive.

Biberach was liberated by the French Army on 23 April 1945. One of the first letters Rosy received was one telling her that her son Jehudi had survived. He was then sent by the Red Cross to Denmark at the time of mass starvation in Holland in the summer of 1945.

This book is moving and uplifting: a cry of pain and hope, and a miracle of survival amid appalling destruction.

Martin Gilbert
14 April 2009

FOREWORD

The year is 1944 and Rosy Kanarek is a 39-year-old woman in Bergen-Belsen concentration camp. During the day, she works for the *Lager Kommandantur*, the camp headquarters. When she is lucky, she collects cigarette ends from her employers and sometimes exchanges them for crusts of bread for Zahava, her nine-year-old daughter who lies ill in the barracks.

At night, Rosy lies awake and thinks about Jehudi, her three-year-old son who is somewhere in Holland in the care of strangers. She also wonders if her husband, Sigmund, will survive for much longer. He is also in Bergen-Belsen and his health is deteriorating by the day.

But despite the fact that Rosy is cold and hungry, and her captors are succeeding in weakening her physically, they cannot destroy her spirit.

Although she never mentions this to anybody, Rosy decides to keep all possible relics of Nazi bureaucracy. Perhaps she thinks that when this nightmare ends – and if she survives – she will tell people about it, because she knows that what she sees every day is beyond belief. Because she is being held in the Star camp, she is permitted to keep a few personal possessions, and so she has one battered suitcase in which she keeps her evidence.

When the war is over, Rosy retrieves all the letters she has sent to her family. She gathers every memento of Nazi brutality, yet she never mentions this to anyone. Life reverts to normality and no one ever talks about the past. Rosy's secret remains hidden for over 60 years – until Zahava unearths her late mother's suitcase.

✡✡✡

In 2006, Zahava Kohn and Ann Rosen meet at a Hebrew class and have coffee together. Somehow during their conversation, it emerges that Zahava was a child in Bergen-Belsen. Over several months, Zahava begins to tell Ann about her early life and they discover that their families knew each other and have been connected for over a century. One day, Zahava casually mentions that her mother – now deceased – had left a case full of papers from the wartime. Until then she had never felt inclined to open it.

Those early conversations mark the beginning of Zahava and Ann's collaboration to piece together the story of *Fragments of a Lost Childhood*. Together they look at the medical notes, Zahava translates the letters and they assemble the fragments. They are both amazed at the amount of material that Rosy, Zahava's mother, had been able to preserve and wonder how she managed to do this under the most terrible – and perilous – circumstances.

They can never be sure why Rosy remained silent about having this material, but Zahava does know that her mother never wanted her family to be victims. Her overriding objective was for them to grow up unburdened by the past. So the suitcase had remained closed – perhaps because Rosy knew that if it was unlocked, the spell would be broken; and if the old wounds were opened, they might never heal. But wherever Rosy went, the suitcase went with her...

For Zahava, revisiting the past was not easy. The process of confronting memories that had been buried for so long took tremendous courage, but she resolved to undertake this project – for two reasons: to honour the memory of previous generations and to answer the questions of those who would come after.

When Ann first visited Zahava, she had no idea that this book would be the result. Looking back, she can only reflect on the privilege it was to embark with Zahava on this voyage of discovery and to share so much that was personal and precious.

ACKNOWLEDGEMENTS

Fragments of a Lost Childhood would never have been researched and written without the support and input of all my family, particularly my husband Ralph and my eldest daughter Hephzibah, whose ideas and encouragement persuaded me to undertake this project. Love and warmest thanks also go to my daughters Michelle and Maxine for their helpful comments and advice as the book progressed. I also felt it was important for my grandchildren, Alex, Talia and Theo, who mean the world to me, to be able to read my story and perhaps understand what happened during the Holocaust.

I should like to extend my sincere thanks to Ann Rosen, who has used the content of our conversations to write a coherent and very readable account of my early years, skilfully and sympathetically piecing together the evidence from the many documents collected and preserved by my mother.

I should also like to express my special gratitude to the distinguished historian Sir Martin Gilbert for writing the moving introduction to this book.

Warm thanks also go to the Smith Family and the staff at The Holocaust Centre for their input, and for the wonderful and critical work they do. May I also express my gratitude to Wendy Whitworth, who edited this book with great sensitivity and sentiment. Her wisdom and guidance are manifest throughout the book.

Finally, I dedicate this book to the loving memory of my parents, Rosy and Sigmund Kanarek, without whom the documents and photographs would never have existed.

Zahava Kohn,
August 2009

In piecing together Zahava's story, I have been immensely grateful for the support and help of many people. Above all, I have been conscious that the memory of the Holocaust cast a long shadow on many of the people around me.

As the daughter of refugees whose immediate family miraculously escaped the Holocaust, Zahava's story has a particular resonance for me. In the course of my research, I made the chilling discovery that many members of my grandmother's family were gathered at the same collection points and herded onto the same trains as the Kanarek family, but ultimately met a different fate. Today, all we have to remind us of them is a date and place of death.

We could never have produced this book without the support of The Holocaust Centre, Beth Shalom, and I feel personally indebted to the Smith family for their remarkable vision in creating the Centre. I would also like to thank Wendy Whitworth, our editor, who has guided us with wisdom and kindness through every stage of this project; and Glen Powell, for his advice and skilful design.

My thanks also go to the following organisations for the use of photographs and documents from their collections: The United States Holocaust Memorial Museum, Washington; The Bergen-Belsen Memorial; and La Société Jersiaise, Jersey.

I could not have written Zahava's story without the very special influence of my parents, Aron and Ruth Vecht, whose own lives were very much shaped by the events of the Holocaust. Thanks also to my husband, Stuart, for his incredible support and to our children, Joshua, Gavriel, Netanel and Yoel, for making it all worthwhile.

Ann Rosen
August 2009

Zahava, aged two

BEGINNINGS

Like most of those who lived through the Nazi era, survival for me has always meant moving forward. I was never encouraged to look back and for most of my life I never wanted to. But today, when I look at my nine-year-old granddaughter, Talia, it seems unbelievable that I was just a little girl like her when my happy childhood came to an abrupt end.

In the first few years of my life, I spent time in several countries – Palestine, Switzerland, Germany and Holland. Since the memory of my early years is very hazy and there is no one left who can verify many of the details, I am left with the task of piecing together the story of my early childhood from the documents and photographs that I discovered in the summer of 2006. My mother had passed away five years earlier, but the existence of material documenting the family history lay undiscovered for over 60 years. It is only very recently that I have decided to reflect upon those early years and try to recall what I remember of that time.

My father

My father, Salke, known as Sigmund (Sigi) Kanarek (23 June 1904 – 3 October 1976) was born in Poland, but went to live in Düsseldorf at the age of four. Sadly, his mother had died shortly before his *Bar Mitzvah* and his father had married his late wife's sister, as was often the custom at the time. My father's family was religious; he also received a good general education, leaving school around the age of 18.

My mother, Reisel, known as Rosy, née Guttmann (5 October 1905 – 6 July 2001) was born in Nowy Sacz, a town on the Czech/Polish border. Her family went to live in Zürich, Switzerland, when she was around five years old. The Guttmann family were Hasidic and cultivated. I remember my maternal grandmother clearly – she always had her head covered in strict accordance with the Jewish laws of modesty. She spoke flawless German and had elegant, perfect handwriting.

My mother

As well as running a traditional Jewish home, my grandmother was employed as a sales representative for a clothing company. She travelled to remote Swiss villages selling thermal undergarments. She also helped my grandfather who worked importing cigars. I was always impressed by the range

3

of her talents and her versatility. Despite coming from a sheltered, very religious family, she knew how the world worked and had life skills that might have been considered exceptional for women of her time.

The Guttmann family was linked to the Sanz sect of Hasidic Jews. I was frequently told that my great-grandfather was the *shochet* (religious slaughterer) to the *Divrei Chaim*. That was said to be a great honour, because the *Divrei Chaim*, who was the leader of the Sanz Hasidim, was renowned as a great *Talmid chacham*, an outstanding Torah scholar.

My mother was an emotionally strong and intelligent woman who had been encouraged by her parents in her early education and in music. She had many talents and played the piano and sang beautifully. After leaving school, she had attended commercial college. She would have liked to further her education and study medicine, but her father would not permit this. At the time, university would have been thought to be potentially too secular an influence for a girl from a religious home.

The culture in which my parents were raised was strictly Orthodox, and it was not acceptable for young men and women to mix freely. By the time my mother met my father, she was 27; and her family was delighted that she had met her match. Prior to meeting my father, I think that she probably helped out in her father's cigar importing business, but exactly how she spent the years after the completion of her education and prior to her marriage is not entirely clear.

I know that she was introduced to several local young men who were thought to be appropriate, but she found none of them to her liking. She was said to be an attractive and well-liked young woman. Eventually, a *shidduch*, (an introduction to a potential partner) was

My parents, Rosy and Sigi, on their wedding day

arranged with a young man from out of town. This was likely to have been the result of suggestions from other family members or rabbis who knew the Guttmann family. My father travelled from Düsseldorf to Zürich several times to meet my mother and her family. After a few months they decided to get married.

My parents were married on 16 February 1932, in Frankfurt. This was chosen as a good location that suited both families, as it was between Zürich and Düsseldorf. Their marriage took place at Breuer's synagogue. The photographs from that time show both my parents looking radiant and splendidly attired – my father in top hat and evening dress, my mother in a long, fashionable robe holding a bouquet of fresh flowers. They described the wedding to me as a very festive affair with a formal dinner. Members of both sides of the family travelled to Frankfurt to take part in the celebrations.

Hitler came to power in Germany in 1933. With his rise, the half million Jews in Germany were to be set apart from their fellow Germans and denied their right to be an integral part of German life. My paternal grandparents lived in Düsseldorf at the time and, although they were obviously unaware of the full horror of what was to befall European Jewry, the gradual restriction of the rights of the Jews in Germany probably had a significant impact on every aspect of their lives. It was the major influence on the choices my father was to make concerning his future.

From 1933, the political climate in Germany was becoming increasingly antisemitic. In that year, the boycott of Jewish businesses began. This was followed by progressively more and more restrictive laws targeting the Jews and limiting their economic and social freedom. Consequently, the level of emigration increased dramatically. In fact, in the early years of Nazi rule, Jewish emigration was permitted and even actively encouraged. From 1933 to 1938, half of the Jewish population left Germany. My parents were among the 33,000 Jews who chose to leave Germany for Palestine. At the time, it was still under the British Mandate.

My parents' reasons for going to Palestine in 1935 were certainly to escape the persecution that Jews were experiencing in Germany. Yet they were also very idealistic and, like my father's family, they were members of *Mizrachi*, a religious Zionist group founded on the idea of establishing a Jewish state in Palestine. Some members of my father's family had left for Palestine prior to the Nazi rise to power. They were among the early Zionists who sought to establish a state where Jews would be free to live and practise their religion without fear of persecution.

My parents planned to leave for Palestine immediately after their wedding, but had to wait for official papers. This was obviously a lengthy and bureaucratic process. Consequently, they were in Amsterdam from February 1933 until sometime in 1935 when they were finally able to leave.

My father had two brothers, Bernhard and Hermann (Zvi), who were already living in Palestine. As far as I remember, they worked on the establishment of *Tirat Zvi*, an early religious kibbutz. These early pioneers established self-sufficient communities based on agriculture.

My father's sister, Mirjam, also immigrated to Palestine in 1935, prior to the outbreak of the war. She later married Abraham Hirsch in 1937, who was originally from Duisberg in Germany and had moved to Düsseldorf. I believe that he was among the Zionist pioneers who received some training in agriculture in Europe prior to moving to Palestine, where they were involved in the establishment of the kibbutz *Chafetz Chayim* which started in Kfar Saba. Later, he was appointed to a senior position in the *Agudah* in Palestine. (*Agudah* was an international Orthodox Jewish organisation). As later correspondence will show, he used his influence to attempt to secure my parents' release when they were sent to Bergen-Belsen.

The remainder of my father's family were still living in Düsseldorf. However, in the first half of 1938, numerous laws were passed restricting Jewish economic activity and occupational opportunities. On 28 October, 17,000 Jews of Polish citizenship, many of whom had been living in Germany for decades, were arrested and relocated across the Polish border. The Polish Government refused to admit them, so they were interned in "relocation camps" on the Polish frontier. Among these were my father's brother, Moshe, and his young family. In February 1939, through his connections within the *Mizrachi* movement, he managed to obtain travel documents for Palestine, so fortunately, along with his wife and two young children, he was able to escape from Europe.

My parents were probably optimistic when, in 1935, they left Holland for Palestine as they had planned. By the time they were finally able to travel, my mother was at a late stage of her pregnancy with me.

By all accounts, they were both thoroughly delighted with the event of my birth in Ramat Gan, Palestine, on 5 August 1935. I remember them talking about the well-known German doctor, Professor Zondek, who had delivered me. The Zondek brothers, Hermann and Bernhard, were eminent Jewish physicians in Berlin, who, despite huge contributions in the field of German medicine, were dismissed from their posts in Berlin by the SS in 1933. Professor Zondek had apparently joked with my mother that I was the prototype – a sample of a perfect baby. He advised my mother "to have a dozen more!"

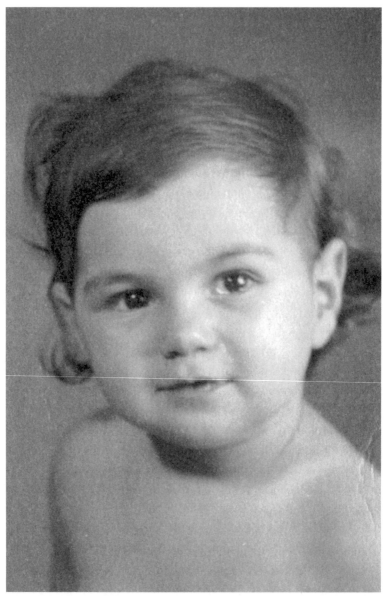

Zahava, aged one

I was named Zahava after my father's mother, who had died when my father was 12. My grandmother was called Golda, a Yiddish name which means golden and obviously implies someone precious. Since I was born in Palestine, my parents opted for Zahava, the Hebrew translation of Golda, which they thought to be more appropriate for the time.

The move to Palestine must have been something of a challenge for my mother. Once they settled there, life was undoubtedly very difficult and they struggled to acclimatise in an unfamiliar environment. When I reflect on what my parents endured to try and make life a success in Palestine, I am impressed by their determination.

I remember that my mother told me that they were fortunate in renting a very comfortable apartment, with heating for the cold winters. My parents enthusiastically invested in new furniture that was appropriate for their new life.

At first my father tried to work selling leather goods. My mother's brother, Edy, had a very successful business in luxury leather goods in Europe and hoped that my father could make a living by selling his merchandise in Palestine. However, they soon discovered that there was no market for luxury goods there. Having worked in sales and in a European business environment, my father was then employed in manual labour for the first time in his life. I believe he worked on building projects for Solel Boneh, the main construction company in Palestine at the time, which is still an important building company in modern Israel. Although my father was always naturally industrious, this must have been something of a trial for a man who was neither cut out for, nor trained in, this field of work. The climate was very different from that of Europe and my mother found it very difficult to cope with the extremely hot weather.

There was also the security problem. My mother was mainly at home with me. But on the few occasions that she had to take me to the clinic, my father would wait anxiously until she returned safely on the bus, since raids and attacks from the native Arab population were a frequent occurrence.

Zahava, aged one *Rosy and Zahava in Palestine, 1937*

It is interesting to look at the photographs from 1937, which paint a somewhat idyllic impression of our life in Palestine. In one particularly memorable shot, I appear as a healthy well-fed child, enjoying my time in a tin bath on the balcony of our apartment in Ramat Gan on a sunny day. In another photograph, my mother looks slim and well dressed by my side. The reality behind her smiles was very different. Unfortunately, the climate made my mother seriously unwell and she became severely dehydrated. Consequently, she lost a significant amount of weight and became very weak. Her poor health meant that remaining in Palestine was impossible. On medical advice, my parents were urged to return to a cooler climate.

They had both very much hoped to make a success of life there, as many members of my father's family had done before them. It must have been a devastating blow for them to have to return to Europe, but obviously they felt they had no choice. My parents left Palestine on 28 April 1937. I was one and a half at the time. But the fact of my being born in Palestine under the British Mandate turned out to be fortuitous, and later was an important factor that contributed to our being saved from transportation to Auschwitz.

It is not clear what my parents' plans were at this stage. From the documents and photographs of the time, it is evident that they spent time in Switzerland, and even visited Germany, between returning from Palestine and deciding to settle in Amsterdam once more. It is possible that they had hoped to be able to settle in Switzerland where my maternal grandparents were living, but were prevented from so doing by the rigid Swiss restrictions on immigration.

By this time in 1937, anti-Jewish laws were already well established in Germany. The Nuremberg laws, which effectively took away the rights of Jews as German citizens, had been in place since 1935, and consequently my parents were unable to return to my father's home town of Düsseldorf. They decided to go back to Holland and settled in Amsterdam. They probably chose Amsterdam because of its familiarity to them and the quality of Jewish life there. Many German Jews had moved to Holland in the 1930s and at the time it was thought to be a safer place for Jews than other parts of Europe. It is quite likely that my parents saw this as a temporary move. In Amsterdam my father found work in the Jewish-owned rainwear company where he had been employed in 1933 as a sales representative.

His employers, Mr and Mrs Haskel Rubin, were also family friends who became very significant in helping our family in the years prior to and during the war.

My father's identity papers documenting his return to work in Amsterdam, 1937

Zahava and her mother in Palestine, 1935

On the beach in Palestine

Rosy and Zahava with Edy, Esther and Marianne Guttmann, Zürich, 1937

Zahava and her mother, 1937

Zahava, 1937

Rosy and Zahava, 1937

Zahava and her parents, 1938

Zahava and her cousin Zahava, Düsseldorf, 1938

Zahava sitting at Lies's attic window

CHILDHOOD

My memories of childhood are patchy, but I remember a general feeling of being a happy and secure child. I was only a toddler when we left Palestine and between 1937 and 1940, I spent time in Zürich with my maternal grandparents, to whom I was very close. We also visited my mother's sister, who lived in Antwerp, and we travelled to Düsseldorf to see my paternal grandparents.

In those early years, I have no recollection of being aware of the turbulent political situation in Europe. Perhaps my parents deliberately shielded me from the harsh realities of the outside world. I do not know why my father's parents remained in Germany when their children had all left for Palestine, and living as Jews in Germany was becoming ever more difficult. It is possible that they were unable to escape. In the late 1930s, it became yet harder to find a way out. Many people encouraged their children to leave, but were themselves left caring for elderly relatives and were eventually trapped.

From a young age, I was often ill. Initially, I had recurrent tonsillitis and middle ear infections. I remember that visiting the ear, nose and throat specialist – Dr Fernandes – was a regular occurrence. From around the age of four, I developed asthmatic tendencies.

I have early memories of being sent to Switzerland for convalescence, to breathe the clear mountain air. There are pictures of me, aged four, at a children's nursing home on Mount Rigi, near Lake Lucerne. I also went to Zandvoort on the Dutch coast. I know that during this trip I was with Mr and Mrs Kapper; they were the aunt and uncle of our neighbour, Lies de Betuwe, and I recall taking long walks along the seafront with them.

Zahava, aged four, on Mount Rigi

Zahava with children from the nursing home in Switzerland, summer 1939

My parents were very sociable and had many friends. They were both loving, but expected me to be disciplined and I had a routine and fixed bedtimes. I'm sure that as a child I went to other children's houses, but I have little memory of this because few of my childhood friends survived the war, so my recollection of them has somehow been wiped out. I do remember playing with one friend – Jupie van Dyk. Her father was a lawyer and her family had a beautiful house that was very close to where we lived.

From the age of around four or five, I attended the Jewish Nursery School in Amsterdam. A memorable photograph from that time shows a happy group of toddlers posing in Dutch national costume. There is a huge collage of a windmill in the background and the girls are wearing Dutch bonnets and caps, and the little boys are dressed up similarly.

After nursery school, I attended the Palache School for a short time. This was the Jewish primary school located close to our home in the centre of Amsterdam. My teacher there was Mr de Goede. Saul Sohlberg and Jupie van Dyk were in my class at the time. They were both in hiding in Holland for the duration of the war. Fortunately, both survived and they later married each other. Today they live in southern Israel.

There was also a boy from my kindergarten, Lex Aronson, who was later killed fighting for the State of Israel. Apart from them, I have no clear recollection of my other classmates, but a photograph of the period shows my school class. Most of the children are wearing yellow stars. Since wearing these was compulsory, I can only assume that in the cases where the stars are not clearly visible, the children were wearing them on their outer garments, which do not appear in the photograph. I remember that my mother was always particular that all the corners of the star had to be sewn down firmly,

Zahava at nursery school in Amsterdam, back row, 3rd from right

Zahava at the Palache Primary School, Amsterdam, back row, far right. Not all the yellow stars are visible.

but as a child, I was blissfully unaware of the symbolism of the yellow star or of the stigma attached to this label.

Our apartment in Amsterdam was situated in a Jewish area where there were many *shtiebels* (small prayer houses). It was on the first floor at 14 Nieuwe Achtergracht and was modern and well-equipped. It had running water and a shower – facilities that were considered very comfortable for the time. My parents had returned from Palestine with all their furniture – which was more suited to Palestine than Europe; for example, they had sofa beds that needed to be set out every evening.

Ours was a hospitable home. Domestic life revolved around preparing food and my mother was preoccupied with this. She was very caring and kind and tried to help ladies from the community who were in need of money, so from time to time before *Shabbat*, the Jewish Sabbath, one lady came to make *lockshen* (noodles); someone else came to make the *challah* (*Shabbat* bread). My mother would pay them for their services and this was her way of helping them take money home for their families.

I know that my mother used to invite other children round when it was my birthday. I also remember that we had guests for Jewish festivals, particularly *Chanukah* and *Purim*.

As far as I can recall, I used to like going to the Great Synagogue on a *Shabbat* morning. Although I cannot remember who came with me at the time, I have a clear recollection of being beautifully dressed and of wearing white gloves and sitting upstairs in the ladies' gallery. From an early age, I liked decorum and music and so chose the Great Synagogue as opposed to the smaller, more informal prayer house that my father favoured. He attended the local *shtiebel* regularly. My mother did not come to synagogue with me on *Shabbat* mornings – she was often busy at home preparing for guests.

Among the few people I remember from my early childhood is the singer Leo Fuld. As a young child, I remember sitting happily on his lap as he sang to me. He had an extraordinary singing voice and I think his family had hoped he would become a *chazzan*, a cantor. Because of his musical talents, he was able to find work in America and he actually emigrated to the USA just before the outbreak of the war. He became a famous singer of Yiddish songs and went on to sing about the plight of Jewish refugees from Europe in the 1940s. Sadly, he was one of the few survivors from his entire family.

My father had two cousins who lived in Holland, whose names were Moshe and Callel Kanarek; one lived in Weesp and the other in Amsterdam. Like my father, they had emigrated from Germany to Holland. We used to see them often when they came to visit us, and we would go and see them and their families.

On the third floor in our apartment building, there was a non-Jewish seamstress – Lies de Betuwe. She used to look after me when my mother went out. I enjoyed helping her and she was kind to me.

Another family friend was Leo Fuks, a great scholar with an interest in Hebrew and Yiddish literature. He was a young man of around 30 at the outbreak of the war and I have very fond memories of him. A photograph shows me with him at the botanical gardens in Amsterdam when I was around five years old. This must have been a rare treat and to me this picture is very poignant – it symbolizes the end of the normal happy childhood experiences that were familiar to me until that time. Although not dated, it must have been taken in 1940 or early in 1941, because by the summer of 1941 Jews were banned from all parks and public places.

During the German occupation, Leo Fuks remained hidden in Lies de Betuwe's apartment in Amsterdam. Fortunately, he was

Zahava with Leo Fuks in the botanical gardens, Amsterdam

never discovered and after the war the two were married.

I probably remember both of them well because they were among the few people from my childhood who survived. After the war, Leo Fuks became the Curator of the *Rosenthaliana*, the Jewish library in the University of Amsterdam. He held that post from 1946 until 1971. After the war, he became very well known as he expanded the collection of manuscripts in the library. He also wrote widely about the Hebrew language and about Jewish life in Holland.

✡ ✡ ✡

Zahava with her mother

Zahava with her parents in Amsterdam, 1940

INVASION

From 10 May 1940, the day that Holland was invaded by Germany, conditions became increasingly difficult for Dutch Jews. From that time onwards, many people came to talk to my parents about their plans and possible ways of escaping Europe.

Although I was not yet five at the time, I knew that my parents and their friends were often discussing how they could escape from Holland. My parents spoke frequently of trying somehow to run away to Switzerland. Unfortunately, it was a plan that they were never able to translate into reality. This was probably due to ongoing issues with my mother's health – she suffered a miscarriage sometime in 1939 or 1940 and this must have weakened her considerably.

The Nazis imposed a system of gradual restrictions upon the Jewish population of the Netherlands. To make this work efficiently, and in order to achieve maximum cooperation, they set up the *Joodse Raad*, the Jewish Council, in Amsterdam in February 1941. This meant that they delegated the task of managing the Jews

Order to register with the Jewish Council, March 1941

to members of the Jewish community itself. In this way, the movements of the Jews were monitored from within. One of the early pieces of legislation that they imposed was that all Jews were compelled to register with the Jewish Council and to carry identity cards with them. My mother kept the identity cards from this time.

My mother became pregnant again in late 1940 and my brother, Jehudi, was born on 16 August 1941. It would have been problematic for my parents to travel with a new baby. Besides, by late 1941, there were severe restrictions on the movement of Jewish people within

My father's registration card, November 1941

Holland. There were curfews at night and very strict restrictions on Jews using transport. The only way in which they could leave was probably to be smuggled out at night, but my parents were worried that if the baby made a noise, all our lives would be endangered.

It must have been extremely difficult for my mother to give birth to Jehudi in the middle of the war when our future was so uncertain. I do not have any clear recollections of the event of my brother's birth, although I think that my mother must have spent some time in hospital and that, possibly, I was cared for during some of that time by our neighbour, Lies de Betuwe.

Jehudi was a long-awaited and much loved baby. Yet from soon after his arrival, it became clear to my parents that it was too risky during that time to keep a baby. He was more likely to survive the war if he was somehow separated from the family and hidden. He

Family photographs, December 1941. Rosy, Sigi and Zahava with baby Jehudi

Zahava and Jehudi, December 1941

was blonde and blue-eyed and his Aryan features meant that he did not look obviously Jewish, and so he could be concealed with far greater ease than the rest of us.

The decision to separate from their beloved baby son must have been hugely traumatic for my parents. As a child aged just seven, I clearly recall the day when my mother had to hand my baby brother of just over a year to the care of the Resistance. She was to give the baby away on two conditions: she was not allowed to know where he was being sent since that might endanger those who were caring for him, and she was not allowed to stand near the window or draw any attention to what was happening. I have this feeling of seeing her standing in floods of tears at some distance from the window as she handed over her baby son – not knowing if she would ever see him again.

I believe that the handing over of Jehudi was arranged through my father's employer, Mr Rubin, and contacts between him and the Dutch Resistance. The Rubins themselves had a son, Israel, and a daughter, Fanny. They were hidden in their magnificent canal house in Stadhouderskade throughout the war and fortunately they all survived.

As the net tightened on the Jews who were still in Europe, many people tried to find an escape route. Thousands of European Jews bought travel documents, the majority of which were forged. A number of people were able to leave, and some did escape the Holocaust by fleeing to Central and South America.

Through my maternal grandparents, who lived in Zürich, my parents decided to try to escape by buying papers that would allow the whole family to travel to Honduras. Unlike many people, they obtained genuine travel documents. I am sure that either my grandparents or my parents paid a great deal for these. However,

CONSULADO GENERAL
DE
HONDURAS
EN SUIZA
—
BERNA
—

Mit Eilboten .

Eingeschrieben.

Nº 415. div.1s.

ASUNTO:
Pasaporte.

Bern, den 15. April 1943.

Herrn & Frau Salke Kanarek,

Nwe. Achtergracht 14. I.

A m s t e r d a m .

P.P.

Dem Wunsche Ihrer Verwandten zufolge übersenden
wir Ihnen in der Beilage eine vom Notar des Standes Bern
beglaubigte Fotokopie Ihres Passes No. 538. Der Original-
pass wird Ihnen ebenfalls zugesandt .

Mit dem Ersuchen um Empfangsanzeige mittelst
eingeschriebenen Eilbrief zeichnen wir hochachtungsvoll

Das Generalkonsulat von Honduras

a.A. ein Sekretär : —

Letter from the Honduran Consulate, Bern, April 1943

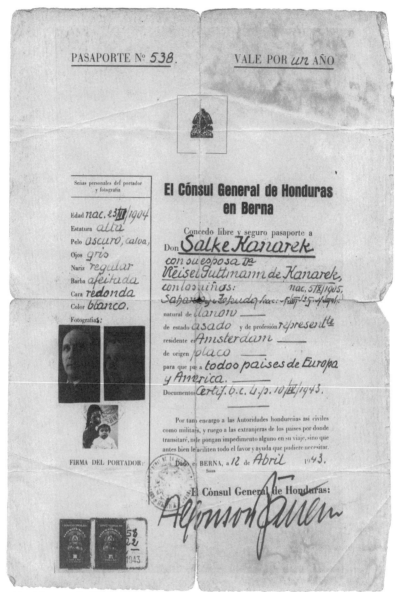

Travel documents for Honduras, April 1943

looking at the documents, it seems that although they had wanted to obtain them far earlier, they actually only received the travel papers for Honduras in April 1943, and this was far too late. By that time, the mass deportations from Amsterdam to Westerbork, that had begun in the previous June, were taking place with ruthless efficiency. Along with the majority of Jews in Holland, my parents were trapped.

Sadly, for my parents and many of those who were with them, the travel documents for which they had paid excessively were never used. At the end of the war, immediately prior to the German defeat, there was a cruel irony in the fact that many Nazis seized the visas that had been the property of their Jewish captives and used them to flee to South America. In this way, they were able to change their identities and lived an untroubled life for many years in a place where the inhabitants were either indifferent to, or ignorant of, their past as mass murderers.

From May 1942, the German Government was authorised to seize all property from Dutch Jews. My father was clearly a man with a great deal of foresight. Knowing that all our property was to be taken from us, he divided it and sent it to various places in the hope of retrieving at least some of it after the war. Among his property at the time was a significant amount of stock from the rainwear company. He also hoped to preserve the family's personal possessions, which were sent to two different locations in Holland. Knowing that all her jewellery would be taken, my mother sewed her wedding and engagement rings into the shoulder pads of my father's suits. It is now clear that my parents also handed over photographs from the pre-war period which today are precious records of their pre-war existence and of a world that vanished with the arrival of the Nazis. The photos record, albeit in a fragmented form, my early, happy childhood years.

With the benefit of hindsight, it is gratifying to see that most of the people that my father chose as custodians of our possessions proved themselves to be truly loyal and trustworthy. The letters that survive are a testimony of this and show that there were some ordinary Dutch people who remained principled, even in the face of Nazi tyranny. For the majority of Jews who returned to their homes after the war, the situation was far more bleak and they were not able to retrieve any of their property.

Zahava and Jehudi, December 1941

Deportation of Dutch Jews to Westerbork
© *United States Holocaust Memorial Museum*

DEPORTATION

The large-scale deportations of Jews from Holland began on 14 July 1942. As a child of almost seven, I remember being aware that there were problems. I think my parents tried very hard to shield me from what was happening and, as I was often ill, I was probably in my bedroom a fair amount of time and so did not hear much of the adult conversation. But I did have an awareness that Jews were being rounded up.

On 26 May 1943, the SS came to our apartment. I was in bed, very sick with chickenpox. We had heard that the Germans were coming to take all the Jews, who were to be gathered together in the main square – Jonas Daniel Meijerplein. People said that they would not take me because I was ill. The SS were famously neurotic about the possibility of being contaminated by infectious diseases, so we hoped that since my chickenpox was very severe, this might deter them, or at least delay my deportation. Unfortunately, their determination to carry out orders in a thorough and efficient manner was even greater than their fear of contamination.

The SS officers suggested that they would take me separately on a special transport for the sick, and that my parents would meet me later. Although I had always been a biddable and agreeable child, this suggestion provoked an uncharacteristically strong response. At the thought of being separated from my parents, I started screaming loudly in a totally uncontrollable way. I absolutely refused to go alone. Because of my hysteria, and not wanting to unsettle the orderly evacuation process, in the end the SS agreed to take me with my parents. As I recall, they gave us some time to pack – just one suitcase for each person. I think that my parents helped me to dress. We all dressed in as many layers as possible to take with us as many clothes as we were able to wear. We were informed that the SS would return and escort us to the main square.

The fact that I was never separated from my parents was particularly significant and may well have been our saving, because since I had been born in Palestine when it was under the British Mandate, my legal status differed from that of my parents – I had British protection. This was to have an effect on all the decisions that were made concerning our subsequent treatment at the hands of the SS.

Amsterdam's main central square was packed with people of all ages and we were escorted there with our three suitcases by the soldiers. I felt very ill and worried about how I would manage to keep standing upright. We were left to stand for a few hours until they sorted us out. We were then taken by ordinary train to Westerbork. I have no recollection of the journey.

My parents had obviously anticipated our deportation. They had asked a neighbour to inform my maternal grandparents, the Guttmanns in Zürich, in the event of our being forcibly removed from our home. Late in June 1943, my grandparents received this postcard:

27 May 1943

Dear Guttmann family,

    Your postcard of 17th May has not reached your children. Unfortunately, they were taken yesterday on 26th May 1943 – that means Rosy, Sigmund and Zahavi. Should I hear anything about them, I will let you know immediately. Julchen [Jehudi] is in good health. In the circumstances, he is alright.

In the name of your loved ones,
Warmest regards,
L. Schochen

This card was very important since it conveyed the vital information that my grandparents had needed – that we had been taken away. The writer also conveyed the fact that Jehudi was in good health and no longer with the rest of the family, although my grandparents were clearly already aware of this. The signature on the card, L. Schochen, is not a name with which I am familiar. But it is likely that the writer was using a code that my grandparents would understand. The name *Schochen* is a transliteration of the Hebrew word *shochen*, which means neighbour. I think that although our neighbour Lies de Betuwe probably wrote the card, it is likely that Leo Fuks gave her the idea to sign it this way.

Zahava, aged seven

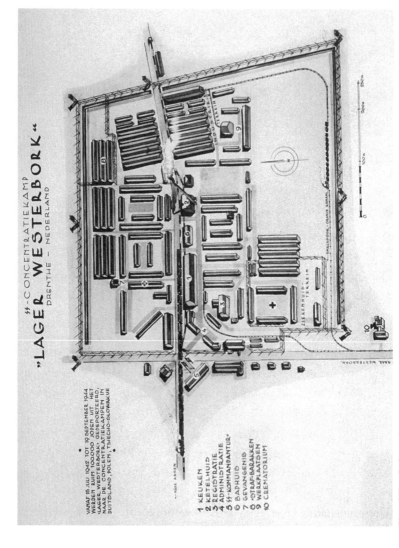

Plan of Westerbork transit camp
© United States Holocaust Memorial Museum

WESTERBORK

Westerbork camp was originally set up in 1939 by the Dutch Government in Holland to accommodate refugees, who had escaped Nazi persecution in other European countries. The costs involved in caring for the Jewish refugees were met by the Jewish Refugee Committee. After the Germans took control of Holland in 1940, they decided that Westerbork ideally suited their purposes and transformed it into a transit camp for the Jews before what was euphemistically referred to as 'resettlement in the East'. In this way, Westerbork was transformed from a place of refuge for Jews to a staging post in their final journey.

From June 1942, Westerbork was active as the main transit camp to which most Dutch Jews were taken before being sorted and selected, and later transported to their almost certain deaths at either Auschwitz, Sobibor, or, less commonly, to Bergen-Belsen or Theresienstadt. Over 100,000 Jews were sent through Westerbork. In addition, about 6,000 Jews were deported to concentration camps from other locations in Holland. There was also a smaller transit camp – Vught – from which Dutch Jews were transported to concentration camps in Germany, Poland and Austria.

Members of the Ordedienst, *Jewish police, directing a transport of Dutch Jews*
© *United States Holocaust Memorial Museum*

Most people were at Westerbork for a short time – a few days or weeks. From May 1943, my parents and I were there for nine months. My father worked throughout our time there. I am not sure what his work involved, but he was required to report for work at set times every day. The inmates of Westerbork were employed in menial tasks. Some were sent to work on local farms, but control of the movements of those incarcerated there was strictly monitored. My mother, too, was put to work.

Although I do not remember discussing the nature of my parents' work there, my mother managed to keep some of the work cards from that time. From these records, we can see that she worked sorting scrap metal at one time and sorting out beans and pulses at another.

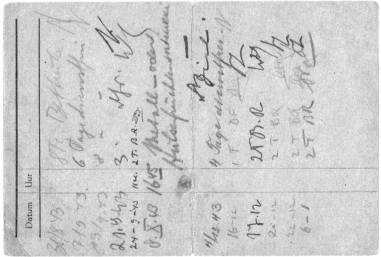

Rosy's work card from Westerbork

The following note shows that my father was given some specific task for two days in September 1943, but the nature of the task is not noted here.

20 9 1943

Kanarek Salke

Barracks 64

Has permission during the period from 20 9 43 to 21 9 43 to stay outside his own Barracks in order to perform his urgent and official duties.

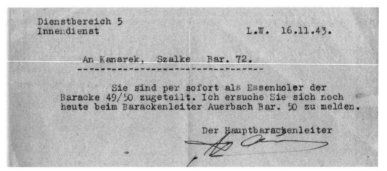

This note below dated 16 November 1943 shows that he was required to distribute food. Here he is also in a different Barracks – 72 – whereas previously he was in Barracks 64.

Kanarek Salke

Barracks 72

16 11 43

You are immediately allocated as 'food fetcher' for Barracks 49/50. Please report today to barracks leader Auerbach, Barracks 50. Head Barracks leader

At Westerbork, there was a semblance of ordinary life. We were even supplied with a laundry list, although I am sure there was no possibility of actually making use of this service! People worked and waited. The Jewish Council was forced to run the camp and this helped the Nazis to keep up the façade of normality. It was a way of ensuring that camp life ran smoothly, with minimum opposition and conflict.

My parents received several letters while they were at Westerbork. It is quite likely that these were sometimes accompanied by food packages and there is evidence that some of the food packages did get through to them.

Lager Westerbork Wäscheliste		Lager Westerbork Duplikat Wäscheliste	
Wäsche No.	Bar.	Wäsche No.	Bar.
Name:		Name:	
Anzahl Fam. Angeh.		Anzahl Fam. Angeh.	
Datum der Abgabe:		Datum der Abgabe:	
Oberhemden		Oberhemden	
Kragen		Kragen	
Unterhemden		Unterhemden	
Unterhosen		Unterhosen	
Combinations		Combinations	
Schlafanzüge		Schlafanzüge	
Nachthemden		Nachthemden	
Damenhemden		Damenhemden	
Schlüpfer		Schlüpfer	
Büstenhalter		Büstenhalter	
Waschlappen, Lätzchen		Waschlappen, Lätzchen	
Handtücher		Handtücher	
Kleine Tücher		Kleine Tücher	
Badetücher-mäntel		Badetücher-mäntel	
Bettücher		Bettücher	
Bettbezüge		Bettbezüge	
Kopfkissenbez.		Kopfkissenbez.	
Tischdecken		Tischdecken	
Deckchen		Deckchen	
Taschentücher		Taschentücher	
Einzel-Strümpfe		Einzel-Strümpfe	
Overalls		Overalls	
Arbeitsmäntel		Arbeitsmäntel	
Schürzen		Schürzen	
Stückzahl zusammen.		Stückzahl zusammen.	

Sämtliche Wäschestücke sind deutlich lesbar zu numerieren. Aushändigung der Wäsche erfolgt nur gegen Vorlage des Duplikats.

Laundry list from Westerbork camp

The following letter was sent by my grandparents in Switzerland to my parents. Clearly, my grandmother was very anxious about the situation in Europe and the likelihood of our deportation to a concentration camp, although she could not express this openly. This letter, in which she conveyed the fact that she was actually ill because of stress, was sent to our apartment in Amsterdam. Ironically, by the time it arrived at our address, we had already been deported.

Although not all of the content of this letter is clearly legible, it is concerned mainly with my grandmother's attempts to send food packages to various people. It is possible that my grandparents were sending food to Mrs Roodenburg as a sort of payment for the care of my brother, Jehudi. Mrs Roodenburg was connected with the Dutch Resistance and knew something of his whereabouts during the war. This was also a coded way for my grandparents to let my parents know that they were still in contact with those involved with Jehudi's welfare. The letter was forwarded to my parents in Westerbork by our neighbour Lies de Betuwe.

19 May 1943
My Dear Children,

As you can see, I received your card yesterday. As I now have Chaskel's address, I have written to him, and he should write back immediately, and he should be good enough to send one [parcel] now and one on Sunday, and then another three a few days later. It is the same price whether two or three are sent.

Today I ordered a parcel of sardines containing fourteen boxes for Mrs Roodenburg. It takes a long time to get there. There is nothing else to be sent at present.

What's new? Are you all well? I need to recuperate. The circumstances have been bothering me very much. I do not sleep at night. The doctor told me today that it is all because of my nerves. I believe that good news from you would be the best medicine for me.

Lots of kisses,
Many kisses for the little ones,
Mama
Many, many thousand greetings and kisses, Papa

The following letter from Lies de Betuwe, our friend and neighbour who remained in Amsterdam throughout the war, reveals

51

something of the fear experienced by ordinary Dutch people during the occupation.

Although at this stage there were already shortages of fresh food, Lies was still able to buy some basic items for us and send them to Westerbork. I don't know whether the parcels she sent ever actually reached us.

In her letter she alludes to the fact that our flat had been looted and our remaining possessions stolen. Clearly, she does not want to add to my parents' worries. But the *visitors* to whom she refers must have caused her great anxiety since she knew that by hiding a Jew, Leo Fuks, in her attic, she was putting her own life in danger.

Towards the end of the letter, she refers to visiting a friend about *the little dress*. I cannot be sure what this really means, but I don't think that in the circumstances my parents would have had any concerns about a little dress. Lies was possibly making a coded reference to checking about my brother Jehudi's well-being. She was one of the few people who knew about his situation and she was also in regular contact with my grandparents in Switzerland.

5 June 1943

Dear Rosy and all,

Your card was received and I have sent off a parcel. There is one package of oats, a parcel of rice, barley, split peas and a small packet of Hopjes [coffee sweets]. Write if you have received it. Then I will send you some bread. How are things otherwise?

I was happy to hear that you were able to remain at Westerbork. How is the dear child? Can she acclimatise to it yet? I thought it was so dreadful.

How are things with [your] uncle?

First of all, the acquaintances who have stayed here, send their best regards. I hope that the Landaus are also still there.

*I won't tell you too much about your apartment. I have often had
visitors [the SS]. Now I've put a large bolt on the door, but it does not
help much. I'm not allowed to complain.*

*I have received mail from your mother three times, but how can I send
them on to you? I have written to her directly and am waiting for a
reply.*

*I have been to this friend about five times for the little dress and have
not yet had a reply. It is a pity; perhaps I will send someone, or have
you got an address that I can go to?*

*For us it is terrible – so quiet. I don't like to be out in the street now.
Now I will stop writing. Be healthy and strong.*

Yours,

Lies,

A little kiss for Havi

Mrs Roodenburg also managed to contact my father directly for
the first time in June 1943. This letter must have been a great source
of comfort to my parents:

Amsterdam

16 June 1943

Dear Mr Kanarek,

*I have not received any news from you so far. I would like to know
your barracks number and I should very much like to hear if the food
parcels arrive. I will wait to send you the cocoa until then. Is it possible
to inform me of the arrival of parcels? I have received messages from
other friends. I know Mr B Samuels in Barracks 70 very well, perhaps
he could talk to you.*

Here all is going very well. I hope to hear from you soon.

Many regards to your wife and little girl.

Very best wishes,

A C Roodenburg

Today another parcel was despatched.

From the day of our deportation from Amsterdam, when I had severe chickenpox, I was ill for much of the time in Westerbork.

Zahava's sick notes, signed by Doctor Nussbaum in Westerbork, 1943

Later during our stay, I had debilitating headaches and was told I had contracted meningitis. Since virtually all the Jews of Amsterdam were deported to Westerbork, there were many doctors among those imprisoned with us. From the records that remain from this time, it is clear that I was cared for by Jewish doctors, who were known to my parents. I think that Dr Nussbaum was our doctor prior to our deportation and his name is on one of the fragments that we still have. It is likely that my recovery from these life-threatening illnesses was a result of the attention and dedication of these doctors, who were working in conditions that were far from ideal. I have no recollection of where I was treated and whether I was put into a separate unit from my parents during my illnesses.

People were sent to Westerbork as complete family units. Since all the adults were forced to work, the problem of how to keep the children occupied had to be addressed. I remember that there were lots of children in Westerbork. Some people made an effort to brighten up our days and occupy us – I don't know if they were told to do this officially or if they did it on their own initiative. Hans Krieg, a German Jewish inmate in the camp, organised a choir for the children. I remember him as a large, cheerful man who always wore a beret. We used to sing songs with him, which I enjoyed. I can even remember the words of some of these songs. I have vague recollections of performing for the adults in the evenings as a way of passing the time and in the hope of lifting the mood. There was also a lady there – Lotte Bio – who was a teacher. She tried to organise some kind of lessons and activities for us.

Although there were efforts to make life seem normal for us, our existence in Westerbork was obviously very strange. I was aware of the fact that we were all there against our will, surrounded by barbed wire and constantly guarded, with no possibility of escape.

I don't think I knew the destination of the trains that left Westerbork every week. But I am sure that the adults who were there knew of the full horror that awaited them. Many of the inmates were German refugees and had already seen brutality on a scale that the Dutch Jews had not yet fully experienced. Every Monday night, lists were circulated of those who were to be transported on the following day. On Tuesdays, there would be the dreaded transports to the East and the atmosphere in the camp would be subdued and silent.

My father was a deeply Orthodox man. In the camps there was very little opportunity to commemorate Jewish festivals, yet my father always kept the fast days. In particular, he fasted on the 17th of *Tammuz*, as that was the date in 1943 when all the great rabbis and Jewish scholars were transported from Westerbork to their deaths. Throughout his life he kept this fast day.

At this stage, our living conditions in Westerbork were tolerable. I think I was in a bunk bed with my mother. We were given some food and a few Red Cross food parcels were getting through to us, possibly from my grandparents in Zürich. At Westerbork, there was still the possibility of receiving mail. A month after they were deported, my parents received this letter from Mr Jelles, a fireman who worked at the fire station close to our flat in Amsterdam. Shortly before we were taken, my parents had entrusted some of their possessions to him.

22 June 1943
Dear Mr Kanarek,

It was a great pleasure for me to hear that you are still in Westerbork and I sincerely hope that your wife and daughter will soon be completely better, and I hope that you will be allowed to stay in Holland for quite some time. If you are able to, I would very much like to have the opportunity to hear from you about what you most need. Also, if you

have any cooking facilities there, then I could think about that when
sending the next parcel. Through circumstances, I have not been quick
in replying to you, but I assure you that this was not due to negligence on
my part. We have had some bad experiences here in the last few days,
but please be assured that in the future, I will write to you much more
quickly. In the meantime, I have no more news to write to you.
Best regards and a speedy recovery to you all,
From the Jelles family
PS Special regards to your wife and little daughter. To my great regret,
I was not in a position to say goodbye to you when you left.
Again warmest greetings.

From this carefully worded letter, it is clear that the situation in
occupied Holland was becoming more risky for Dutch people. It is
not exactly clear what the *bad experiences* Mr Jelles alluded to were.
Long before the mass deportations took place, those who were
opposed to the Nazi regime were sent to Mauthausen concentration
camp. To me, the implication of this letter is that ordinary people
knew what was happening to the Jews. Mr Jelles was happy that we
had remained in Holland as there was a general feeling that we
would remain relatively safe while on Dutch territory.

Mr Jelles' letter tells us that although we had only been in
Westerbork for a month, both my mother and I had already been ill.

A month later, we received another letter from Mr Jelles. My
parents had been asking for certain items to be sent. Fresh fruit was
obviously scarce and my parents were keen for us to have adequate
nutrition. Infestation with lice was already a problem at the camp,
hence the request for the special comb.

21 July 1943
Dear Mr Kanarek,

As I sent a parcel to you this afternoon, I would just like to send you a little note and I hope that you receive this in good health. We have received your card and I thank you for that. It was a great pleasure for us to learn that your wife has started to make a good recovery and we hope that she will soon be completely recovered.

You wrote to us asking for some fruit, but at the moment, this is really very difficult. I have looked everywhere for lemons but I can't get them. I have sent some grapes, but I am concerned that they have been damaged during transportation. If you could let me know, I would like to know if they arrived and also whether the little comb was what you wanted. I had to look through half of Amsterdam to find it. Next time, my wife wants to try and send you some cooked beans. If you would like that, let us know and we can do it more often. Now I have no further news and, on that note, I'll finish.

Again my sincerest greetings, also from my wife and my children, and especially from me.
J Jelles
PS Give special regards and best wishes to your little daughter.

My parents received another letter three weeks later, this time from one of my father's business associates. From this letter, the horror of what was happening to the Dutch Jews is clear. It also gives some insight into the daily life of Dutch people at that stage of the war.

12 August 1943
Dear family,

We received your letter in good health and gathered from it that your wife has been ill, but is thankfully getting better. On that day, 26 May, my wife was on her way to you, but was not allowed through the blockade. The next day, she went to enquire after you at your factory, but they could not tell her any more, other than that you had been transported to Westerbork. We thought this was worst for Zahavi and Jultje [Jehudi].

A few days later, I went to the neighbours on the third floor to enquire, but they had no news, apart from the fact that you had been taken away.

How is Jultje? We hope he is well. For us things have not improved either. I cannot travel, as we are not allowed to go to the northern provinces. Radios had to be handed over and since last week there have been regular raids. They kept my father for two and a half hours – he is seventy-one years old. In addition to this, there are bombardments. Nowhere in Amsterdam is quiet. We have to be optimistic. Last Saturday, I went to PVZ, the food wholesaler, but he had nothing. At the end of the week I shall try again and, if possible, we will send you something.

PVZ will not be allowed to be a wholesaler for much longer and he presumes that he will have to close his business in September. Then he will be finished as well. That's how one business after another finishes. We received your postcard on 21st of June, to which I replied by return. We heard nothing from you, so we thought that you had been sent away, which now thankfully does not seem to be the case. We have often spoken about you, not knowing that you were still in Holland. We hope that you will receive this letter in health. I will try at the end of this week at PVZ.

Many regards for you all and also from my wife and daughter,
Piet

My parents must have been very dispirited when they spent *Rosh Hashanah*, the Jewish New Year in September, in Westerbork. In addition to worries about my health and our future, they were uncertain of the precise whereabouts of my brother, Jehudi, who was just over two years old by this time.

It is significant to note that the following letter from Mrs Roodenburg was actually written on 30 September, which corresponded with the first day of *Rosh Hashanah* in 1943.

Although she was not Jewish, I suspect she must have known that this was a very significant date for us and wanted to reassure my parents that Jehudi was being well cared for. In this letter, although she does not express it explicitly, it seems very clear that she knows of the fate of those who are transported from Westerbork. Yet despite the desperately sad tone of the letter, she is at pains to reassure my parents that all was well with the nurse and her children. This is a coded reference to Nurse Stol, the lady who was paid to care for Jehudi during this period. *The youngest* child to whom she refers is clearly Jehudi.

30 September 1943
Dear Mr and Mrs Kanarek,

After a long silence, I can write to you again. I am only writing a postcard as I have heard that these arrive more quickly.

All is well with us. All goes according to our wishes, only I am constantly busy. I started writing this card last week, now it is the 4th of October. I have not been able to complete [writing this] due to the disturbances.

You must have been very sorry that Mr and Mrs Samuels have left [transported from Westerbork to concentration camp]. I had also hoped that they would be able to stay in Holland. They were no longer young, but I had hoped that I would see them again. I hope that you will write to me again to tell me how they were.

How are you and your little daughter? I was very sorry to hear that she is not so strong. Maybe by now she is better. I hope that the parcels are arriving safely.

I cannot send anything more through the Joodse Raad *(Jewish Council). This seems to have come to an end. I did not send white beans as I have not got any and cannot obtain them. I still cannot get lemons. At one stage I did get one and sent it to Westerbork.*

All is well with the nurse and her children. I visited them last week.

The youngest is becoming a real boy now – big and really tall, much more of a boy. You may remember, he was just like a little girl with all his curls. That's all. Just keep well.
Many regards, very best wishes.
Was the arrival of Messrs Asscher and Cohen a sensation?
Again best regards,
A C Roodenburg

At the end of this letter, Mrs Roodenburg refers to the arrival in Westerbork of Abraham Asscher and David Cohen. These two men had been very prominent, wealthy and influential Jews before the war. In February 1941, the German authorities gave them the terribly difficult task of forming the *Joodse Raad*, the Jewish Council. Both were of the opinion that it was necessary to comply with the German authorities in order to obtain concessions. However, there was widespread disagreement over this view within the Jewish Council and the wider community. It is known that the Germans were given lists of members of the Jewish community by the Jewish Council and Asscher and Cohen were held to be responsible for this.

It is also noteworthy that Mrs Roodenburg mentions that the *Joodse Raad* was now no longer in existence. It had functioned as a means of sending food to those who were deported and was an efficient way of centralising and organising the mass deportations for the Germans.

In May 1943, 7,000 of the Council's staff were deported and many were sent from Westerbork straight to their deaths. By 29 September 1943, the remaining staff were deported and Asscher and Cohen were sent to Westerbork on one of the last transports from Amsterdam. Both survived the war and returned to the Netherlands afterwards. The post-war Dutch Government and the community of survivors raised serious accusations against Asscher and Cohen.

For that *Rosh Hashanah*, 1943, while we were in Westerbork, I made a New Year's card for my parents. It was lovingly written and constructed from a disused cardboard carton. I still have it today as a memento of our time there.

Rosh Hashanah *card made from disused cardboard box, 1943*

Dear Parents,

I hope that next year we will be in better circumstances. In the meantime Shana Tova Veticateivu *(Happy New Year, and may you be inscribed in the book of life.)*

Although I was eight years old at the time, I had received very little in the way of formal education, and I suspect I would have needed help with the spelling. I think this card must have been made at one of our makeshift classes, where coloured pencils and other basic materials were provided. It is decorated in bright colours with a *shofar* (a ram's horn), a star of David and a honey pot.

During our time in Westerbork, my grandparents in Switzerland were living in a state of incredible anxiety concerning the fate of their two daughters. In addition to our situation, they were terribly worried about their younger daughter, my aunt Miri, and her family.

Miri Erdman, my mother's sister, had been deported with her husband, Yechiel, from Antwerp to Drancy, the transit camp near Paris. Their son, Juleke, was a toddler at the time and had been removed from the transport by a clergyman. Juleke was then sent to Switzerland. He was an only child and was in an extremely distressed state, having been separated from his parents at such a young age. He was cared for by a Gentile family in Switzerland and although they were kind to him, he was deeply unhappy. My grandmother, who was neither young nor in good health, was very concerned about her three-year-old grandson. He was taken to visit my grandparents regularly, but they were not able to have him living with them because of their health and because of my grandmother's work.

My grandmother was still working as a sales representative for a clothing company and was making every effort to earn money despite her poor health and wartime shortages. She travelled widely in an attempt to find new customers. The following letter was written on one of her many train journeys in Autumn 1943, just after the end of the festival of *Succot* (Tabernacles). My grandmother had received our card on *Simchat Torah*, an especially joyous festival in the Jewish year. However, her emotions were far from joyful when she sent this letter, in which some of her worries are evident.

Although I am not sure of the precise identity of all of the people to whom she refers in her letter, she was trying to find out more about the fate of her daughter, Miri, and her son-in-law, Yechiel Erdman.

Zürich
25 October 1943
My Dear Children,
   Just to let you know that thank G-d, we are well and hope to hear the best from you. We received your card from the 12th on Thursday, just as I was leaving [to go to the synagogue] for the hakafot *[procession around the synagogue to celebrate the annual completion of the reading of the Torah].*
   Dear Juleke went home [to those caring for him] yesterday. He wanted very much to stay with us but unfortunately, that is not possible.
   What's new with you? I won't write any more about it to Bauer. He has sent it to the Jewish Council so there is no point in bothering him further. When I have spare time I will phone Emmy.
   Have you got warm clothes to wear? Have you got woollen blankets? It's early in the morning and I'm on the train. That's why I am writing to you quickly.
Many kisses for darling Zahavi,
Your devoted mother,
Many thousand kisses. Peace should come soon,
Papa

It seems that only a small amount of the mail and food packages sent to my parents actually reached them in Westerbork. My mother was in contact with her cousin, Regina (Rex) Hermann. Although none of the letters sent by Regina to my mother from this period seem to have survived, below is a letter that my mother sent from Westerbork to Regina, who lived in Stockholm at the time.

Westerbork
9 November 1943
My Dearest Rex,
  We received your letter (dated 23rd September 1943) with the photo on 29th October. As you can see, this took a long time and we were so happy to receive it. Though I do not know your husband, it seems to me that your little one looks like you. Unfortunately, I do not have a photograph of us here, so I cannot reciprocate, and there is no possibility of having one taken. Hopefully, peace will come soon and we can meet again.
  Thank you for taking such trouble to send us something. Unfortunately, so far nothing has arrived, but thank G-d, we are not starving. Thank G-d, we are fine and hope to hear the same from you.
  Why do you write so little?
  Our Zahavi is eight years old now and has two long black plaits, just as I had. No further news for today.
  Lots of love and kisses and all the best,
  Yours, Rosy

At this time, we had been in Westerbork for almost six months. My mother's comment that *we are not starving* was probably true.

By now, it had been over a year since my mother had handed over my brother to the Resistance. During this time she did not know where he was, or what his fate would be.

One day, however, she received a bag of raw haricot beans. She was puzzled as to why she had been sent this package. Throughout one night, she went through the bag of beans. Hidden among them, she discovered this small photograph of my brother, Jehudi.

Through this coded message, she knew that her child was alive

Photograph of Jehudi that was concealed in the bag of beans

and being cared for. Later, in Bergen-Belsen, she managed to keep this photograph as a symbol of hope. I think that throughout the bleakest times, she held out the hope that one day she would be reunited with her beloved son.

We had been in Barracks 64 at Westerbork for some months when, one day, both my parents were called in for cross-examination by the notorious Fräulein Gertrud Slottke, who had been brought in specially by the SS for this purpose. I do not remember her precisely, but I do recall that the mere mention of her name terrified my parents. She is remembered by other survivors of Westerbork as a cold, heartless woman. Her role for the SS is recorded as "administrative". Gertrud Slottke was in charge of the lists of inmates at Westerbork. She was to determine the camp to which we were sent – and it was on her whim that the fate of thousands was decided.

Prior to the interrogation, I was woken by my parents in the middle of the night and told that if I was asked what had happened to Jehudi, I had to say that I had been ill and I didn't know what had happened to him. Somehow, he had been lost on the way. My parents knew that if the SS discovered that my brother had been hidden, it could be catastrophic for all of us. The official papers had a picture of me with my brother as a baby, so my parents were extremely worried. However, for some reason, I was never cross-examined. No questions were asked about the baby in the picture. For years afterwards, my parents would talk about how incredible this was and how it proved to be the saving of all four of us.

My mother and father were informed of the outcome of their cross-examination by Fräulein Slottke. They were scheduled for the next transport bound for Auschwitz. The decision was irrevocable. Their friends in Westerbork despaired, realising that if even my parents were not given preferential treatment, no one would be.

I had seen the cattle trains earlier. Fearing that I would not be able to breathe in them since I suffered from asthma, I asked my parents if, when we had to travel, we could go very early to the trains to get a better place. There were usually two or three regular carriages with windows and seats for the SS. Somehow my mother had to convey to me that things were not going to be quite like that.

My parents had many friends in Westerbork and they all decided as far as possible to try to stay together on what they thought would be their final journey. They were scheduled for the transport to Auschwitz, but suddenly when we were on the platform, a Dutch official came with a message for them. "Mr Kanarek, I have instructions that you are to be removed with your wife and child from this transport." He said that he wished he had similar messages for other people.

We will never be sure what prompted this message and our removal from the transport bound for Auschwitz. Since I had been born in Palestine when it was under the British Mandate, we had what was considered to be special status. We were supposed to be 'protected'. This meant that we were potential 'exchange prisoners'. We could be used by the Nazis as bargaining pawns to be exchanged for German prisoners. But my place of birth had been documented previously, so it is not clear why we were first selected for the Auschwitz list, and then removed from it. It is well known that the Nazis were keen to fill their 'quotas' with specific numbers for lists to the various final destinations. At Westerbork lists were drawn up every week and people took desperate measures to have their names removed from these fatal lists.

Meanwhile, my grandparents were trying to secure our release and made many appeals through various channels in an attempt to save us from the horrors of Auschwitz. The following documentation, which was sent to Westerbork from the Jewish Council, is evidence of their efforts.

Jewish Council, 20 June 1943
Department of Emigration
Mr Salke Kanarek 23 06 04
Mrs Reisel Kanarek Guttmann 05 10 1905
Kanarek Sahawa 05 08 1935
Temporary Camp Westerbork
We confirm that after investigating the documents you produced, we have put you on the list recommended for exchange to Palestine and have supplied your name to the Swiss Embassy in Berlin, who are dealing with the appropriate authorities.
Yours faithfully, Department of Emigration
Administration No 34

Name

Verwaltung, Bar. 34.   No.:

Name: **Kanarek**
Vorname: **Salke**
geboren: **23. 6. 04**   Bar.: *72*
Familienangehörige:
mit Ehefrau und Kind

Ihr Antrag vom: **4. 7. 43**
Entscheidung:
**Sie werden für den Palästina-Austausch in
ein anderes Lager überstellt werden. Die
eingereichten Unterlagen erhalten Sie an-
bei zurück.**
          1 Anl.

Datum: **22.11.43**   Kontrolle:

DR. 2 Verwaltung
Antragstelle

Kanarek
First Name   *Salke*
Date of Birth   *23 06 04*
Family Members   *Wife and Child*
Your application of *4.7.43*
Verdict
You will be transferred to another camp for the Palestine exchange.
Other documents submitted are returned herewith.
Date 22 11 1943

The timing of this message – that we were to be removed from the transport destined for Auschwitz – was miraculous. Had my father been called a few moments later, we would have been on the crowded train and probably impossible to find. The train would have moved off and we would have faced an entirely different destiny.

My mother, father and I were taken back to the barracks in Westerbork, while all my parents' friends were sent to Auschwitz in cattle trucks. Many prominent people from the community were on that transport, but nothing could save them.

One of the most poignant mementos among my parents' documents from their time in the camps is the following coupon:

Food coupon, Westerbork

From Jewish Council, Amsterdam
Department of Assistance to people leaving
Valid for grocery parcel which will provide provisions for three days.
People who are called for work. This packet will be given in exchange
for this coupon in the camp of Westerbork on the day of departure. Only
one card per person will be given.

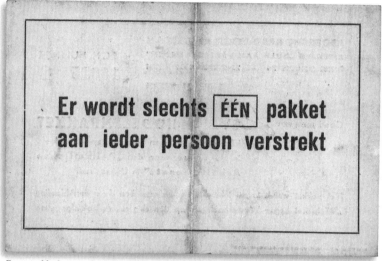

Reverse of food coupon from Westerbork

Since this coupon is not dated, it is not clear as to when my parents received it. The most likely scenario is that it was given to them after they were selected for Auschwitz, but because they were not actually sent there, they were never given the opportunity to exchange the coupon for food and therefore were able to keep it. The other possibility is that coupons like these were given to all prisoners as they left Westerbork for their allocated concentration camp. But this seems less likely, since if they had been able to exchange it for food, they surely would have done so, and then would not have been able to retain the coupon.

To me, this coupon reveals the pathetic position in which the Jewish Council staff found themselves. They were totally powerless to do anything to prevent the mass deportations and to save their people. Yet they still attempted somehow to find a way to provide the community with provisions for their final journey.

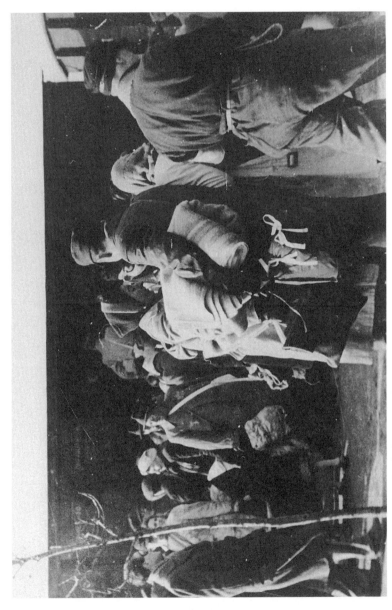

The deportation of Jews from Westerbork to concentration camps
© United States Holocaust Memorial Museum

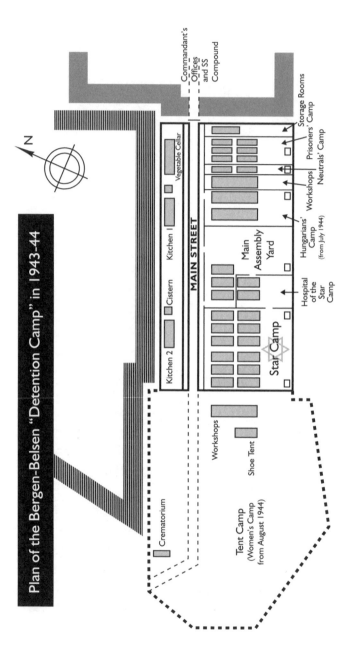

Plan of Bergen-Belsen camp

BERGEN-BELSEN

The long wait was over; having been held at Westerbork for nine months, we were now to be relocated to Bergen-Belsen. I do not remember the journey, nor do I recall my parents' reaction to the events surrounding our 'transfer'. But other Dutch Jews who made the same journey remember being taken as third-class passengers on ordinary trains, so we were clearly being treated in a different way from our friends who were taken to Auschwitz in sealed cattle trucks.

Ours was one of the first transports to go to Bergen-Belsen from Westerbork and it is quite possible that my parents did not know anything about this camp. We travelled via Hanover, Northern Germany, to Celle near Bergen-Belsen.

This was considered to be preferential treatment as there were no gas chambers there. Bergen-Belsen was more of a slow death camp, while Auschwitz was an extermination camp, a factory of death – people were murdered within hours of arrival. In Belsen, inmates were put to work. People died of illness, starvation and disease, but the process was slower and less certain.

Ironically, although 50,000 civilian inmates and 50,000 Russian prisoners of war died there, the Germans originally set up Bergen-Belsen in April 1943 as an *Aufenthaltslager*, a holding camp. Its purpose was to hold prisoners who were suitable for exchange with the Allies for German citizens.

Clearly, there was some value in the distorted minds of the Nazis in keeping a workforce in Belsen alive. This is documented in a decree from Heinrich Himmler to Lt. General Muller regarding Hitler's wishes in 1943: "They are to work in such conditions that they remain healthy and alive. These types of Jews are valuable hostages for us." The booklet published by the Bergen-Belsen memorial site explains that the original intention was that around 30,000 Jews should not be deported to death camps. Instead, they were to be retained for exchange purposes. In reality, only a few hundred inmates from Belsen were released and exchanged.

We arrived in Bergen-Belsen in January 1944. On arrival, the men and women were put into separate barracks and I remained with my mother. We still had the possibility of meeting my father sometimes.

We were held in the 'star camp'. This was where many of the Dutch Jews who might be eligible to be exchange prisoners were kept. The star camp meant that we had to wear a yellow star on our ordinary clothes, rather than wear camp uniforms. Although we did not realise it at the time, our conditions were slightly less horrific than those of the inmates of other parts of the camp. We were also allowed to keep some of our personal possessions with us and this is how my mother was able to save some of the documents from that time.

My father had to work. Together with hundreds of inmates, he worked in the reconditioning of old shoes that the Germans had seized from the Jews and the inhabitants of countries they had occupied. The work that the inmates were made to do consisted of unstitching the seams of old shoes and cutting out pieces of leather that could still be used. The work was filthy, physically demanding and unpleasant. In true Nazi fashion, records were kept of the number of old shoes collected and the amount of work done by each inmate.

A huge pile of victims' shoes at Bergen-Belsen
© United States Holocaust Memorial Museum

At some stage, all my father's teeth were knocked out. I did not know how this had happened, but I was constantly worried that something would happen to him. I remember the watchtowers with searchlights. I was terrified of the dogs and the guns. I also recall hearing the name of someone we knew; he was summoned to report somewhere and his name was called repeatedly. I knew then that something bad had happened to him and that he had been killed. I wasn't sure how this had taken place; no one had explained it to me and I probably thought it best not to ask. I felt a general sense of fear that was constant, yet never expressed.

My father slept in Barracks 12 with the other men, while I shared a top bunk of three with my mother in Barracks 18. I had asked for this position because I felt I could breathe more freely high up. I often remained alone in bed during the day. During my 13 months in Bergen-Belsen, I was ill with jaundice and hepatitis. These illnesses had begun in Westerbork, but I was never taken to a hospital. I think my mother always wanted to keep me close to her. Often, she would explain that I was too sick for roll call and she would take the soldiers to show them how ill I was. My memories of my time in Bergen-Belsen are somewhat hazy, but one particular memory that is clear in my mind is the endless and pointless roll calls that would go on for hours and hours, even in the snow. I attribute some of the rheumatic problems that I have today to standing in the snow as a child, without adequate footwear.

Apart from these endless early-morning roll calls, there was no fixed activity for me during my time there. The only other significant events of the day were the distributions of 'food'. We existed, rather than lived, on the most appalling and inadequate rations. We were given a drink of dark water – which was meant to resemble coffee – in the morning, together with a tiny square of thin stale bread. I think that in the evening there was something that was meant to be soup. It was a watery substance, which sometimes had bits of horse meat and root vegetables floating in it.

I have a childhood friend who was with me in Bergen-Belsen. She clearly remembers commemorating her *Bat Mitzvah* in the camp. This rite of passage, when a Jewish girl reaches the age of 12 and traditionally enters adulthood, is usually a time of celebration. To mark the occasion, my friend's family had collected all their food rations and she was given two whole pieces of bread.

Because we were starving and becoming increasingly weak, we

were all obsessed with the subject of food. I remember that my mother would speak to the other women about the foods they all used to enjoy in their previous life. They spent hours fantasising about food and exchanging recipes in an effort to keep up their spirits. It was a bizarre form of escaping the horror that surrounded us.

In Bergen-Belsen, I saw people in a terrible state, yet I started to accept it. From a very young age, I saw extraordinary things and took them for granted. There was a boy in our barracks who was around eight years old. He was with his mother, who was sick and very distressed. She kept on saying in German, *"Heinz, gib mir das Messer"* (Heinz, give me the knife) because she wanted to commit suicide. I can still hear her saying this. She would be crying these words again and again, pleading for someone to put an end to her misery – it was terrible. I think that eventually my mother took the knife away.

While we were in Bergen-Belsen, it is quite clear that efforts were being made to try to secure our release. My uncle Abraham Hirsch, who was the husband of my father's sister, Mirjam, lived in Palestine. A few 'exchange prisoners' had managed to leave Belsen for Palestine and had related the full horrors of the camps. So Uncle Abraham had no illusions about our possible fate, should his attempts prove unsuccessful.

Meanwhile, my maternal grandparents were desperate for our release. They did not know precisely what had happened to my mother's sister and her husband, Miri and Yechiel Erdman, but they feared the worst. It was thought that they had been taken to 'the East' and nothing more had been heard from them.

The following letter is from my uncle, Abraham Hirsch, who was head of World *Agudah* in Palestine, to my maternal grandparents, the Guttmanns in Zürich. It shows how actively he was working to secure our release.

Jerusalem, 1 08 1944
Dear Mr Guttmann,
*I have received your letters of 11th May and 28th June and thank you
for them. You probably received my telegram of 26th July 1944 in which
I let you know that Salke Kanarek and family are in Bergen-Belsen,
Celle, near Hanover. The barracks number of Salke is number 12 and
the barracks number of Rosy is 18. Both are well with their children and
in possession of Palestine documentation. People who came here in the
last exchange to Palestine (who left there at the end of June) have told
us that Salke is working in a shoe workshop locally, and that Rosy works
for the* Lager Kommandantur, *the camp headquarters.*

*If it is at all possible, it would be advisable to send them food parcels.
I would advise you write to Salke, Rosy and family via the Red Cross
at the above address. People who came from there have told us that post
does arrive.*

*We have also cabled to London in the meantime with our request that
they should be included in the next exchange. As Salke is rather young,
one cannot be sure that he will really be exchanged. In any case, here
we shall try everything possible and with G-d's help, we shall succeed.*

*In connection with the subject of exchange, I would urge you to apply
to the Red Cross, as one suspects that the Red Cross has some influence
in the creation of the exchange lists.*

*At the same time, it would be advisable to write to the Swiss government
as protectors of British citizens in German custody, and request that
Salke and family should be put on the exchange list. The number of the
certificate is M/438/43/D/216 and it was forwarded on 6th October by
the Government of Palestine to the British Foreign Office in London.*

*I should like to ask you again to let us have any news of Salke and
family as soon as you hear anything. I will also keep you posted constantly.
With best regards to you and your family,*
Yours, Abraham Hirsch

This letter is interesting as my grandparents knew that Jehudi
was in hiding, and it is likely that my uncle also knew of this.

However, here Abraham Hirsch refers to *'their children'* in his letter to them, probably hoping that all the family could escape to Palestine.

We had been in Bergen-Belsen since January 1944. I am sure that my mother would have tried to send regular cards to her parents, but clearly these did not always reach their destination.

None of the cards sent from Bergen-Belsen that we still have today reveal anything about the privations and the terrible life we were living at the time. In fact, they seem to have been written to a precise prescribed formula. I am not sure of the exact conditions in which my mother wrote these. However, my guess is that either they were scripted by the Nazis, or the fear of writing anything other than the official line dictated the format.

The content of the following card is particularly noteworthy. My mother writes that, "*We are healthy.*" Among the tiny fragments from Bergen-Belsen concerning our health, it is clear that my father was given permission to have bed rest from 7-10 August 1944. The medical records of the time show that from 10-24 August 1944, I was very seriously ill.

19 August 1944
Dearest Parents,
  Just to say we were very happy with your greeting. We are healthy
and also hope to hear the same from you. We can receive food parcels
here, but not registered parcels.
Love and kisses, Rosy, Sigi and Zahavi

It is interesting to note that my grandmother writes to my parents
for *Rosh Hashanah*, the Jewish New Year, on 10 September 1944. The
implication in this card seems to be that she has not heard from them
for ten months since they were deported to Westerbork. My mother
had sent a card three weeks earlier, but clearly that had not yet arrived.

10 September 1944
My Dear Children,
  We were very happy with your card. It is exactly 10 months since you
wrote to us from Westerbork. We are, thank G-d, fine, and hope that all
is OK with you. I have ordered food from various sources to send to you.

*I hope that you will receive it.   I have written to Mrs Roodenburg and
I have thanked her very much.   For the coming new year, we wish you
all the very best.*
Heartiest greetings and kisses, Your devoted Mother

It is evident that all letters were heavily censored.   My
grandmother's mention of Mrs Roodenburg and her gratitude to
her was clearly connected with the welfare of my brother, Jehudi.
Obviously, she could not state this explicitly.

My grandmother wrote to us very often.   The cards written in
the autumn of 1944, around the time of the Jewish festivals, had a
particular poignancy for her.   We were used to spending the Jewish
New Year and all the main festivals with my grandparents in Zürich.
We had always enjoyed attending synagogue with them and were
very moved by the beautiful services that were led by my grandfather.
My grandmother was obviously sending food packages at the times
of the festivals, fully aware that we were unable to observe any of the
religious practices that were such a fundamental part of our tradition.
This card was sent on the eve of our festival of *Succot* (Tabernacles).

1 October 1944
My Dear Children,
    We are well and hope also to hear the same from you. We have sent six parcels to you through the Red Cross, also some from other places. We hope that this time you will receive some of these. We hope you are inscribed for a good year.
Lots of regards and kisses, Your devoted Mother

The following card from mid-October 1944 shows that although we had been in Bergen-Belsen for ten months, my grandparents had received only two postcards from us.

16 October 1944
My Dear Children,
    Today we received the second postcard from you. We are very happy to hear that you are well. We are also well. We have already sent you many parcels and please G-d you should receive them all.
Our good wishes and kisses, Mama

Two months later, my mother was able to write to her parents:

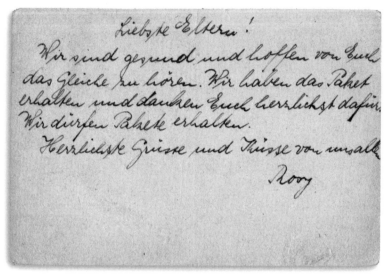

14 December 1944, Block 18
Dearest Parents,
We are healthy and hope also to hear the same from you. We have received
your parcel and thank you very much for it. We are allowed to receive parcels.
Warmest greetings and kisses, Rosy

One day, my mother received a special parcel. This was unheard of in Bergen-Belsen. Often my parents would have to sign to say that they had received food parcels that never reached them and were obviously intercepted by the Nazis. The parcel was a honey cake and the sender was Mrs Roodenburg of the Dutch Resistance. We knew that she was in contact with the people caring for Jehudi. So the fact that the cake came directly from her was understood by my parents as a coded message that Jehudi was well.

It is clear that during our time in the camp, our living conditions became increasingly difficult. At the beginning of our stay, there were some washing facilities within the barracks. But during our time there, more and more inmates arrived and the SS crammed more beds into our living space. After a time, the only toilets and water available to us were outside, and most of us were too weak to be able to reach the facilities. Consequently, disease spread quickly within our barracks. I remember the sense of squalor and yet despite all of this, my mother did her very best to care for me in the way that she had always done.

Since many of us were too ill and weak to go out and use the latrines, we improvised and used tins as bed pans, which were kept on the beams above the beds. One such tin was used by a very sick woman who had typhus. One day, she inadvertently knocked the tin over me. I had long plaits which were now soiled and my mother was in a terrible state. She was desperate to wash my hair. She was beside herself at the thought that I might contract typhus in addition to my other ailments. Consequently, she queued for hours for the dregs of coffee that the SS gave out – because she wanted to wash my hair in it. After this, she still remained determined to keep my beautiful long plaits. They were in a way symbolic to her – whatever destruction the SS had brought upon our family, my mother had to preserve my identity as her cherished little girl.

The fragments of papers that my mother kept from that time show that she was ill and was permitted to take time off work on 12 October 1944.

Sick notes from Bergen-Belsen, 1944

Although not in the best of health during this period, my
mother did manage to work most of the time. Since she worked for
the Commandant, the head of the camp, her employment afforded
her certain privileges. She could collect cigarette ends and then
exchange them for crusts of bread.

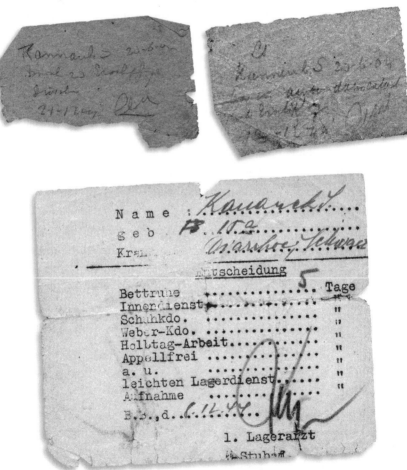

Zahava's sick notes from Bergen-Belsen

My father's health was certainly deteriorating by December 1944. The fragments from 8, 12 and 21 December show that he was suffering from exhaustion and frostbite and was allowed some bed rest. In January 1945, he became even more unwell. These tiny notes from 4, 7, 9 and 19 January record his decline. On 7 January, he was even sent to have a urine examination, although there is no evidence that he received any kind of medication for his numerous conditions.

Sick notes from January 1945, showing the deterioration in Sigi's condition

Although we were kept apart from the other groups of inmates in Bergen-Belsen, they were only separated from us by barbed wire and were able to shout across to us. In January 1945, hundreds of female prisoners arrived from the death marches from other camps, many of them from Auschwitz. It was bitterly cold and even to our eyes, they looked utterly pitiful in their thin, striped camp uniforms. They would call out and tell us of the things that they had witnessed in Auschwitz. They would also sing and cry out aloud in prayer and song. One of my friends, who was in the star camp with me, says that she can still hear their anguished voices singing a verse from Psalms in Hebrew: *"Keli, keli. Lama azavtani?"* (My G-d, My G-d, why have you forsaken me?).

✡ ✡ ✡

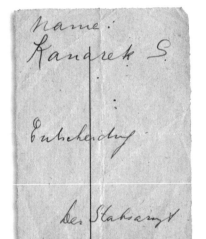

It seems unbelievable that a tiny scrap of paper, on which a barely legible message was written, was actually the ticket for our survival.

On 20 January 1945, a decision was reached and we were told we were to be removed from Bergen-Belsen. This scrawled note reflects the arbitrary way in which our future was decided. I don't think my parents dared to believe that we were to be released or exchanged until it actually happened, so at the time they did not tell me about it or raise my hopes.

I had a great-uncle who was in Belsen with us. His name was Saul Tugendhaft and he was my father's uncle. When my mother heard that we were to be sent somewhere else early, she gathered whatever meagre crusts we had and gave them to my uncle. She said, "Either we won't need them or they won't help us."

Saul Tugendhaft

Sadly, records show that later, Great Uncle Saul was forced onto a transport bound for Theresienstadt as part of the Nazis' clearance of Belsen to make room for survivors of the death marches from across Europe. Sadly, he did not survive the journey and died on the train in April 1945.

With the benefit of hindsight, it seems clear that the decision to allow us to be released from Bergen-Belsen was a pragmatic one from the Germans' point of view. By this time, Bergen-Belsen was terribly overcrowded. There was an urgent need to make room for those who were arriving from other camps. Although it is not entirely clear whether we were exchanged for money or political prisoners, or both, the Nazis were likely to have received something in return for our release.

The transactions that document our exchange give the following details:

19 January 1945: 450 prisoners were selected by the RSHA (Central Office for the Security of the Reich) for 'exchange'. These prisoners held South or Central American *Promesas*.

21 January 1945: 301 prisoners from this selection boarded a Swiss Red Cross train at Bergen. The train consisted of six second- and third-class carriages. The planned travel route was Berlin, Nuremberg, Ulm then Konstanz.

23 January 1945: In Berlin between 124 and 165 of the prisoners were removed from the train to make way for 'more valuable' prisoners, Americans in this case. The prisoners removed were interned in Biberach. Some of the other passengers were taken directly to Switzerland.

BOOK OF REMEMBRANCE

PRISONERS
IN THE BERGEN-BELSEN
CONCENTRATION CAMP

Volume 1

A - K

Kan	Ralph	25.03.1934 Amsterdam	-	-
Kan	Salomon	30.08.1900 -	23.04.1945 Tröbitz	-
Kan	Willi	03.06.1898 Oldenzaal	-	-
Kan	Winnefred	24.02.1931 Arnheim	13.04.1945 Farsleben	-
Kanaka	Jadwiga	- .. - .1880 Warschau	-	- - .03.1945
Kanal	Tauba	10.12.1930 Bendzin	15.04.1945 Bergen-Belsen	-
Kanarek	Salke	23.06.1904 Ulanow	-	-
Kanarek	Zahawa	05.08.1935 Tel-Aviv	-	-
Kanarek	Zuzanna	-	15.04.1945 Bergen-Belsen	-
Kanarek-Gutmann	Reisel	05.10.1905 Neusandez	-	-
Kanarkova	Elisabeth	30.06.1890 -	15.04.1945 Bergen-Belsen	-
Kanataw	Michail	01.09.1911 Koslicha	Horgau	-
Kanbeck	Waclaw	04.03.1905 -	-	22.02.1945
Kan-Brieger	Leonie	29.07.1905 Breslau	23.04.1945 Tröbitz	-
Kandel	Aladar	27.12.1897 Budapest	13.04.1945 Farsleben	-

Page from the Book of Remembrance, Bergen-Belsen, showing the names of Zahava, Salke (Sigi) and Reisl (Rosy)
© *Bergen-Belsen Memorial*

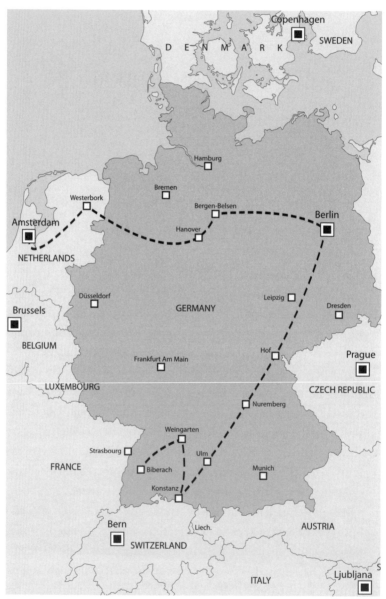

Map showing Zahava's journey from Amsterdam, 1943, to Biberach, 1945

AFTER BELSEN

By January 1945, typhus and other diseases were spreading rapidly in Bergen-Belsen and most of the inmates were starving. From this time, the death rates – which were already high – began to rise more sharply. The arrival of prisoners from other concentration camps caused incredible overcrowding and exacerbated the problem.

I suspect that the decision to move us out of the camp at that time was not due to benevolence on the part of our captors, but to the practical need to make more space. For my parents, there had always been the hope that while we remained in Bergen-Belsen, there was the possibility of our being released or exchanged. A few of my parents' friends had been released in 1944 and, fortunately, because they had papers for Palestine, they had been sent there.

Bergen-Belsen had originally been set up as a holding camp, and as always the SS were keen to maintain this façade. In reality, only a tiny proportion of those held with us in the camp were fortunate enough to be released before the end of the war. Our early release might have been part of this façade by the Nazis to demonstrate to the

Red Cross that they were actually not so terrible and were acting in accordance with their previous intentions.

What prompted the Nazis' decision to let us go at this time will never be totally clear, but I am sure that although we held travel documents for Honduras, and the stated destination of some of our friends in Belsen was Panama, there was never any intention at this stage of the war to send us to Central America! Whatever their motives were, if we had not been included on that exchange list, we would certainly not have survived.

On 21 January 1945, we were among the few hundred 'exchange prisoners' whose names had been selected by the RHSA (*Reichssicherheitshauptamt*, the Reich Central Security Office) and we were fortunate to be placed on a Red Cross transport. Records from Bergen-Belsen show that our train was destined to travel from Bergen-Belsen through Berlin, Nuremberg, Ulm, and then finally to Konstanz.

I remember that there was tremendous relief when we saw that the train on which we were to travel was a passenger train with windows and proper seats. Many of the adults remarked on this at the time. We had become so accustomed to the sight of the cattle wagons – and even I knew that cattle wagons implied something sinister. But because of my fragile condition by that stage, I was not really aware of what was happening or what had been planned for us.

On that transport with us was a friend whom I still see from time to time. She is two years older than I am and was in considerably better health than me when we left Bergen-Belsen. When we discussed our experiences recently, she remembered the journey and recalled "thinking that we were being taken to Switzerland and then suddenly discovering that we were to be interned in Germany, after all".

This is particularly interesting and it is possible that we may have been under the impression that we were going to be liberated at that stage and taken to Switzerland. The train certainly went very close to the Swiss border. Records reveal that the train made several stops on the way and that some of those originally taken from Belsen with us did actually arrive in Switzerland on 25 January 1945.

I do not remember the exact route that we took or much about the journey. By the time I left Bergen-Belsen, I was so weak that I could barely stand up and I had been told to try my best to stay upright; otherwise, the decision to exchange me might be revoked. In the end, I was propped up between my parents and managed to walk onto the Red Cross train that finally took us away from the concentration camp.

I remember the feeling of overwhelming physical weakness on the train. Anyone who saw us knew where we had come from. We looked ill and were clearly starving. Yet the Poles who were travelling on the train lay across the seats so we were unable to sit down. Unfortunately, this abiding memory of the scene has shaped my attitude to the Polish people to this day.

We were taken to a sort of army hostel in Weingarten, not far from Stuttgart. This must have been because of the intervention of the Red Cross. By that stage, I was far too ill to move and so I think I was carried there and then examined by a doctor. My weight was recorded at the time as 23 kg and my father weighed 45 kg. My mother was sure that we were so very close to death that if our release had been delayed even by a matter of days, we would have been unable to endure any more.

Curiously, despite suffering from malnutrition and a host of serious illnesses during my time in the camps, I had grown surprisingly tall. The doctor called me 'the tall girl'. I recall that I was left upstairs in the hostel which became our home for a few days while my parents spoke to Red Cross officials about their experiences.

Most of us were in a very delicate condition, and yet we were so accustomed to starvation and disease that we did not fully recognise the fragility of our situation. There was nobody to give us guidance as to how to acclimatise to eating ordinary food. Having been suddenly released, we were all quite crazy with hunger. I remember sitting at long tables with the other inmates, in what seemed like disused barracks in Weingarten. I have a vivid recollection of seeing one man whom my parents knew, a family friend from Holland. He was sitting at a table, hugging a soup tureen. When we asked him to pass us the soup, he gestured to us to go elsewhere for some.

The following morning, we heard the sad news that this man had died. My parents were terribly upset by his death, which they felt could have been prevented. It was a double tragedy that the deprivation people had endured had reduced them to desperation – and by that stage they were uncontrollable. This man's fate was not uncommon; numerous people died within hours or days of their release. They were so weak and vulnerable after years of starvation that they could not cope with the shock of real food.

Although it is not clear how my grandparents in Zürich heard of our removal from Bergen-Belsen, the news of our release must have reached them by 28 January 1945, as the following letter shows.

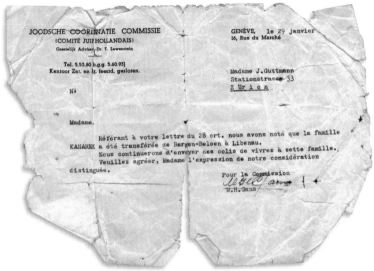

29 January 1945
Jewish Coordination Commission for Dutch Jews
Administrator: Dr T Lewenstein

Madam,
Referring to your letter of 28 January, we have noted that the Kanarek family have been transferred from Bergen-Belsen to Libenau [in fact it was Biberach]. We will continue to send parcels to that family. Sincerely, M H Gans

This letter from a Jewish charity set up in Geneva to help Dutch Jews shows that my grandparents had instructed them to send food parcels to my parents. I am sure that they did this with the very best of intentions, but I have no recollection of ever receiving any of these food parcels.

View of barracks at Biberach internment camp
© *Société Jersiaise*

BIBERACH

After some days in the hostel in Weingarten, we were taken by train to Biberach. This was a large internment camp that had originally been set up for prisoners of war, and people were interned there from a variety of places, particularly the Channel Islands. Yet despite the fact that our freedom was still limited, we were tremendously grateful to find ourselves in circumstances that were a great relief after concentration camp life. We were finally being given food and medical care by the Red Cross.

When we arrived at Biberach on 25 January 1945, we were all still seriously ill. As far as I remember, both of my parents were taken to hospital, which was outside the part of the camp where I was staying. My father suffered from serious heart problems and various other illnesses. My mother had ongoing stomach problems and for all of us, the long-term legacy of standing for hours in the snow for roll call was severe frostbite.

It was during those first few weeks in Biberach, when my parents were in hospital, that a lady called Gerda Hess looked after me. I also remember that a couple from Guernsey – Mr and Mrs Dows – were in charge of the camp and there was a British doctor who cared for me during my time there.

After my mother was released from hospital, we lived in a kind of barracks. My father joined us later, and although being finally reunited should have filled me with joy, I was constantly fearful for my father's health and preoccupied with worries that even after being released, he might not survive.

On 6 February 1945, my mother managed to write to her parents properly for the first time since our release from Bergen-Belsen. This was almost two weeks after we had arrived in Biberach, but I am sure that it must have been the earliest opportunity that she had to write to them. Knowing the extent of her parents' suffering concerning the fate of their family, I can only guess that we were all probably far too ill for my mother to be in a position to write to them in any detail before this time.

In all her letters, my mother does her very best to reflect our situation to my grandparents in the best possible light. Although there was obviously an incredible sense of relief at having been removed from the horrors of Bergen-Belsen, the process of physical recovery was immensely difficult for all three of us. We had witnessed people dying on the trains after release and at various stages en route to Biberach, so my parents must have been very aware of the fragility of our condition. As we saw the suffering of those around us, we were all too aware that survival in those early weeks after being released was still not a certainty.

Although my mother does not mention it in the following card, at the time of writing my father was still in hospital. We were obviously cold and in great need of warm clothing. Along with many of the other survivors, we had problems getting used to a near normal diet after years of starvation. In characteristic fashion, my mother underplays this, but asks for 'some rusks for the little one'.

Her most pressing concern is for friends left to their fate in Bergen-Belsen, who also had relatives in Switzerland and had not been selected for the transport with us. This letter is also interesting since it confirms that despite my grandparents' heroic efforts to send us food packages, in over a year in Bergen-Belsen, we had only received a total of three parcels.

Biberach
6 February 1945

Dearest Parents,

As you can see, we find ourselves in an internment camp. We left Bergen-Belsen on 21 January. Thank G-d, we are fine and we are doing well here. Here we are nursed and in good hands.

If it is not too much trouble for you, I would be grateful if you would send a pair of second-hand shoes for me and Zahavi. One in size 39 and one child's size 36, and a warm dress or sweater for me. Havi does not need anything except shoes and slippers.

Perhaps you could also send some rusks or toast as the little one often has stomach problems.

We would be grateful if you could make enquiries to send us matzot *[Passover bread] in good time.*

Unfortunately, the Holles Rosengarten family did not come [were not on the exchange with us]. Their relatives should take pity on them and do all they can to try and ensure their release. At least, they should receive parcels via the Red Cross. Altogether we received three parcels [in Bergen-Belsen]. Love and kisses, Sigmund, Rosy and Zahavi
If possible, cancel other parcels [to Bergen-Belsen].

At around the same time, in early February 1945, my mother also wrote to her cousin Regina (Rex) Hermann, who was in Stockholm.

Although we do not have that letter, it is clear that my mother also wrote to Rex asking for warm winter clothes. Obviously, suffering from the cold, and with my father still in hospital, this must have been a difficult time for her.

It is clear that at this stage letters still took a very long time to arrive and many were lost in transit. The following letter from Rex to my mother conveys her huge relief on hearing that we had survived Bergen-Belsen.

3 March 1945
My Dear, Dear Rosy,

I was so extremely happy when your card, dated 12 February, arrived at the same time as a card from your mother. [At that stage,] I could not help you, as neither camp nor barracks number were written on it. So now you will receive two parcels, one for Sigmund and one for you. For Sigmund [especially] because he is ill.

Please send Sigmund and Zahavi's camp numbers. As they are not [my] first-degree relatives, you cannot receive large parcels [from me], but you will get margarine, rusks, marmalade, sugar and chocolate, as much and as often as is possible.

You write about a card that you sent me at the beginning of February, but I did not receive this. It is impossible to send matzot *[Passover bread]. In your situation, which is like an emergency, surely you are permitted to eat anything.*

My dear Rosy, I cried from sheer joy when I received this sign of life from you! Just stay healthy. I hope that you will see your parents soon. After the war, I hope that we will have a reunion. Most of all, I hope that Sigmund gets his strength back, my best regards to him.

I have not heard from my dear mother for three and a half months and I am very worried about that.

Please write to me as often as you can and also let me know whether you need any money.
My love and kisses to you,
Yours, Rex

We were fortunate that we had relatives in Europe, living in Sweden and Switzerland – both countries that had remained neutral during the war. Despite this, it is clear that their ability to help us was severely restricted and this must have been a source of great frustration for them.

In the following letter, Rex seems surprised that in spite of all her efforts to send us packages in Bergen-Belsen, none had actually arrived. From her tone here, I think it is quite possible that she wasn't yet fully aware of the truly horrific conditions that we had endured there.

Stockholm

8 March 1945

My Dearest Rosy,

Today we received your letter of 5 February. Unfortunately, I cannot send any clothing. I already tried this in November and again today. I cannot get a licence to do it. I was very sad to learn that you didn't receive any of the parcels I sent [to Bergen-Belsen]. They were sent on 12 November 1944 and on 29 November 1944, always at regular intervals. The last one was sent on 26 February. I am unhappy; I always thought you had received them.

*The place from which these parcels were sent informed me today that
there were other Kanareks on the list. Frank and Joanna Kanarek.
Perhaps you were mixed up with them. Almost all should have arrived;
this is a mystery to me. Please write to me as often as you can. Did you
receive my card of 3 March?*
Lots of love and kisses,
Yours,
Rex
Warmest Regards,
Martin Hermann

During our first two months in Biberach, it is clear that my
mother had several preoccupations. As well as the ongoing worries
about our recuperation, she wrote repeatedly to her parents, yet
received no response. This was obviously bothering her, particularly
since other people at Biberach had received mail. Having finally
been freed from the horrors of the concentration camp, she was
desperate to make contact with her parents – and to find out more
about my brother, Jehudi (Jultje), who would have been four by this
time.

We had all suffered from frostbite, and in the following letter,
my mother is again asking for comfortable footwear to be sent to us,
a request she had first made over a month earlier. I think that in
some ways, this time in Biberach was particularly tough on my
mother. Whereas in Bergen-Belsen all the emphasis had been on
survival and she was not given the opportunity to write about our
suffering to her parents, now in Biberach there was more freedom
and she had time to reflect on the tremendous traumas that she had
endured. In this letter, my mother, who was always an immensely
controlled and practical person, does show some signs of the emotional
distress she was suffering at the time.

Biberach,
14 March 1945

My Dearest Parents,
    We do not know what to think, as we have not heard from you for the
seven weeks since we've been here. Almost all of our friends have
received mail from Switzerland. Mrs Rom's daughter has received a
wonderful parcel with clothing, underwear and shoes, from her brother
in Seefeld Street. Perhaps you could ask them how this was organised.
Lulu Rom received the parcel last week and a postcard on the previous
day. That letter was only in transit for 12 days. We have such bad luck
and are longing for a sign of life from you.
    Do you hear anything from Rex? We have not received a reply from
her either. Have you heard anything from Mrs Roodenburg? How is
Jultje? [Jehudi].
    In case you can send me something, please send some slippers for Sigi,
size 44, Havi, size 37 and me, 39-40.
    No further news from us. Thank G-d, we are fine, although Sigi is
still in hospital, but he is, thank G-d, much better. Last week I got a
good pair of shoes from the Red Cross and Havi got a coat and a
sweater.
Lots of love from all of us and a Happy Yom Tov,
Rosy
Also I wish you a kosher Pesach,
Salke

From the content of my mother's letters, it is apparent that
despite being in an internment camp, my parents were trying to
resume the lives they had led as practising Jews, prior to Bergen-
Belsen. From February onwards, which was seven weeks before the
festival, my parents were concerned about the impending arrival of
Pesach, Passover. My mother might also have felt a particular
longing for her parents and young son at that time as *Pesach* is a

major festival that is celebrated as a family. The strain of living as a fragmented family must have been causing her great anguish.

As Orthodox Jews, we were required to have *matzot*, special unleavened bread, during the entire festival, which lasts for eight days. Since we were no longer starving, my father would have been very particular to try to keep the Jewish laws as far as it was possible in our situation. The challenge of how to obtain these *matzot* is mentioned in virtually all the letters that were sent at this time. In any event, my parents would not have eaten any bread during the festival of *Pesach*.

I am sure that my father's determination to celebrate *Pesach* as fully as possible in the spring of 1945 was particularly significant. More than any other festival in the Jewish year, *Pesach* is the festival which celebrates freedom. At the *Seder* night, we stay up late into the night recalling the story of our redemption from slavery and our exodus from Egypt. *Pesach* celebrates the birth of the Jewish nation and the beginning of our freedom to practise our religion after years of oppression. Having been released from our own slavery and oppression, the symbolism and relevance of our first *Seder* night after Bergen-Belsen must have been immensely moving for my parents.

My mother and father would not have written letters during the festival because on festival days, like the Sabbath, writing is forbidden. The following letter was written the day before the festival of Passover started.

Biberach
28 March 1945

My Dearest Parents,
    Although Sigmund has already written to you today, I would like to write as well. It is just before the holiday, but unfortunately the matzot

have not arrived, but that cannot be helped.

Some people received broken matzot. *We were still hoping to receive some, but are unlucky with the mail from you.*

All my friends have already received several letters, but we have only received the card dated 16 February, to which I have already sent a reply. I hope you received it. Have you heard anything from Edy and family? Thousands of kisses and happy holidays,
Rosy and Zahavi

As my mother mentioned in her letter, my father also wrote to my grandparents on the same day, just before the festival. Despite writing from his hospital bed, he was again preoccupied with the problem of obtaining *matzot*. It is very interesting to note that he mentions that "some *matzot* were baked here" and reflects on how happy he is to fulfil the religious obligation to keep this *mitzvah* (commandment).

I don't know how it was possible for *matzot* to be baked in Biberach, but this seems to be quite remarkable, because obviously attempts were being made to allow us to practise our religion by those administering the camp. It is unbelievable to think that at this stage, during the war, we were living in Germany and yet were able to commemorate *Pesach*, albeit in somewhat reduced circumstances. Ironically, while this was taking place, thousands of our people were being murdered by the Germans because of their religion.

Biberach
28 March 1945

My Dears,
I want to write before the holidays, as I don't know whether Rosy will have time to write to you.
I am still in hospital, but I am getting much better. Today is the start of my ninth week here.

We are very surprised that we have only received a card dated 16 February during the whole period, whereas other people have received much more mail from Switzerland. Some have [at least] received matzot; *they arrived in many pieces, but they have a* kezayis *[the required amount to fulfil the obligation of eating* matzot *on* Pesach*].*

We have also a few matzot *for the* Seder *night. They were baked here and we are very happy. We had still hoped that the* matzot *which you sent would arrive in time. Unfortunately they did not arrive. We also have not heard from Rex. Some friends have received mail.*

Zahavi is going to school and looks well. No further news for today. Lots of love and kisses, best wishes and have a good holiday, Yours, Salke

Although I have no clear recollection of it, there was definitely some sort of makeshift school at Biberach, which I attended for short periods when I was well. It is interesting that my father mentions this in his letter. It was written only two months after Bergen-Belsen and implies that I must have made quite a rapid recovery, yet I am sure that I was still in poor health at this time. However, it is apparent that my father was trying to convey a picture of normality to my grandparents, for whom our situation was a constant worry.

It would have been interesting to have some record of that strange *Pesach* spent in the internment camp in 1945, but I do not even remember whether I was well enough to be part of it. Although my parents were keen to prepare for it, they do not write anything about the *Seder* nights during their Passover in Biberach.

However, my mother does write to her parents during *Chol hamoed*, the intermediate days of Passover. This letter seems to be rushed as it is written shortly before the start of the last two days of the festival, when my mother could not have written. Here her concerns are mainly about the plight of those families left behind in Bergen-Belsen. In fact, she says nothing in this letter about our own condition, but is keen to tell her parents that she has heard from her cousin, Regina [Rex] Hermann.

Biberach
3 April 1945

Dearest Parents,

I wrote to you on Erev Yom Tov, *[the eve of the festival of Passover], when I mentioned that I had not received a reply from Rex. In the meantime, I have received two postcards at the same time from her. She wrote to say that she had sent us two parcels and would take every opportunity to send more.*

Some people have received a few parcels from Sweden. She wrote that she had sent several parcels to Bergen-Belsen...[words crossed out by the censor].

Just received your second postcard dated 16 February – almost fourteen days later, just like the first one. During our nine weeks here, this is the only mail that we have received. You asked about Holles in your last card. I wrote to you immediately that unfortunately they were left in Bergen-Belsen. Her father and siblings should do all they can to get her out of there. At least send packages via the Red Cross. Have you heard anything from Rosy Kleiman? How is Jultje? Is he with Heidi? Lots of love and kisses,

Rosy

This is the last card my mother wrote to her parents before the official end of the war and our liberation. Yet there is nothing in the content of her letter to imply that she was aware that this was imminent. I don't think we had any awareness of what was happening in the wider world. The process of surviving and attempting to recover consumed all my mother's energy completely.

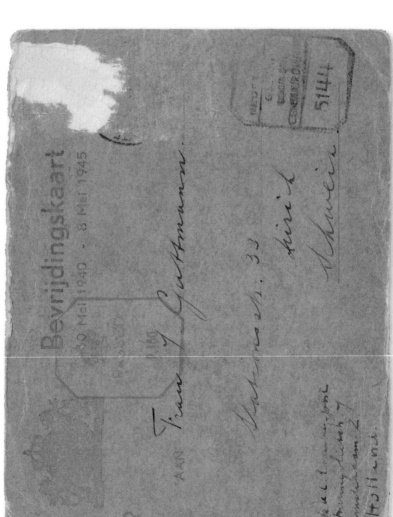

Dutch liberation card, May 1945

LIBERATION

After five years of war, our liberation came suddenly and unexpectedly. I believe that because my mother was so focussed on our recuperation, our liberation came as a huge surprise to her. At the time, our day-to-day survival was her main preoccupation; our precarious situation and my father's health had occupied her for so long that she hadn't even begun to have thoughts or hopes for our future.

I do not know whether my parents had any idea that the end of the war was imminent. Nothing in her correspondence of this time refers in detail to events beyond her immediate concerns. But because her letters were still being censored, it is difficult to gain an accurate picture of the extent of their awareness of the situation in the wider world.

From the card below, my mother is clearly hugely relieved by our liberation. Biberach was liberated by the French on 23 April 1945. She is clearly optimistic and, for the first time, actually expresses hopes for the future.

Biberach
24 April 1945

Dearest Parents,
Mazel tov! *[Congratulations!] Yesterday we were liberated from the Germans. You can hardly imagine how lucky this is for us. Please G-d there should soon be peace in the whole world, and we will finally be able to meet again.*
Until now, it has not been too bad for us in this internment camp, but we have been so spoilt since the arrival of the French – it is difficult to describe – just heaven on earth.
Au revoir, mes chers parents avec mille salutations,
Many thousand kisses,
Rosy and Havi

The final letter that my grandparents received from my mother in Biberach does not add much in the way of information about our condition, but my mother repeats her relief and gratitude that our long ordeal was now at an end.

At this stage, towards the end of the war and in its aftermath, much of the infrastructure of Europe had broken down. As a consequence of this, it is clear that although letters were being sent from my grandparents in Switzerland, they were not getting through to my parents in Germany. This was evidently still a source of concern for my parents.

Biberach
27 April 1945

My Dear Ones,
As we have already written to you, we were liberated on Monday. Thank G-d, we are well. We have no shortage of anything; we just wait for the possibility to be able to see you soon. We are very surprised that

we have not heard from you. We hope the day will soon arrive when we
can hear each other's voices again.
Till then,
Lots of love and kisses, Rosy

About six weeks after our liberation, Mrs Roodenburg, who was in Holland, sent the following card to my grandparents in Switzerland. This historic orange Liberation Card (see p.111), printed with the dates 6-10 May when Holland was liberated from German oppression, must have been received by my grandparents with a tremendous sense of relief. The news that we had survived the camps and that my brother had been well cared for throughout the war must have been overwhelming for them. Throughout the war years, they had prayed for our survival. Yet in their darkest moments, they must have felt that the chances were slim. Now, miraculously, their prayers had been answered and we were to emerge as a complete family after years of separation and suffering.

7 June 1945
Dear Mrs Guttmann,

Now I can write to tell you that your grandchild Jultje Kanarek is in Holland and he is well. We have heard that your daughter and her husband and their little girl are in Switzerland. Is that true? I had already feared the worst. Perhaps the children are already with you? They will be very happy to hear something at last about the little boy. He has grown up well, has not suffered this winter and is chubby and healthy. His appetite was always excellent. He no longer has a little girly face, but is now a real boy and has short hair. He is in a children's home in Haarlem. I haven't seen him for over a year as travelling was not possible. My sister in Haarlem has visited him several times and was very pleased to see him. He is very attached to the woman there and also to his 'little sisters'. This year he went to Kindergarten there.
I hope to hear from you soon.
Many Regards,
Yours truly, Mrs Roodenburg

After our liberation, the plan was for us to be reunited with our grandparents and then, we hoped, with Jehudi as soon as possible. In her letter, Mrs Roodenburg says that she has heard that we are already in Switzerland. I am not sure how long we actually remained in Biberach, nor at what stage during the summer we were actually permitted to travel to join my grandparents. My guess is that we were not yet with them and that we only travelled later in the summer. I am sure that we remained in Biberach for some weeks after liberation. I remember that my parents went out to the local shops and were amazed that there was still food and produce to be bought there just after the war had ended.

When the war was over, there was chaos. We were among the thousands and thousands of displaced people who had been made destitute by the Germans.

After liberation, Biberach changed from being an internment camp to a camp for displaced people (DPs), but the problems of obtaining travel documents and receiving permission to travel were not easily overcome. However, we were in a relatively fortunate situation: we had relatives in Switzerland who were willing to accept us and Biberach was very close to the Swiss border.

For most of our friends who remained in the camp, the trauma was far from over. Although the war had ended, the reality of the devastation it had caused was only just being realised. Many of the DPs had no homes to which they could return as their houses had been looted and repossessed. They had no families with whom they could be reunited as most had been murdered by the Nazis. Their fate was to remain in the DP camp and wait. They were homeless and forced to remain in a country whose army had systematically wiped out their families and consequently, the emotional anguish felt by the Jewish DPs in Biberach was heartbreaking. A friend from that time remembers:

"The war was over... yet we were stuck in Germany. No one wanted us and we had nowhere to go. There was no one to come and claim us. It was the very worst time for me. I could not even begin to imagine a future..."

Zahava, Rosy and Sigi; displaced people, 1945

RECOVERY – 1945

In the aftermath of the Second World War, Europe was full of refugees and displaced people who had lost their homes and families. Many survived the camps only to spend the months and years after the war struggling to find a country that was willing to accept them. Despite everything that the survivors had endured, their plight did very little to awaken the sympathy of most governments.

Few of those who had experienced Nazi brutality had any desire to remain in Germany, and we were among the many refugees who wanted to go to Switzerland. In the turmoil of post-war Europe, we were in a relatively good situation. Our family in Switzerland was active in helping us to be transferred from Germany to Switzerland.

At some point my grandparents must also have come to the sad realisation that my mother's sister and her husband had suffered the same fate as the majority of European Jews and were never coming back.

In the summer of 1945, we left Biberach. This must have been an emotional time for my parents as they parted from some of the friends with whom they had endured so much – Westerbork, Bergen-Belsen and finally Biberach. At that stage, we didn't know where we would end up living and what might happen to our friends.

Since we were fortunate in having living relatives, we were able to leave Biberach relatively soon after the war. Others remained there until late 1946, when they were finally able to travel to England. The majority of DPs, though, faced several years of life in internment camps.

From Biberach, my mother, father and I went to St Margarethen, a town on the German-Swiss border. This move, organised by my grandparents, was an intermediary stage for us for a few weeks before we were allowed to join them.

I know that my grandparents were helped by a cousin called Eugen Messinger, who held some sort of government post in Switzerland. He pleaded with the officials that

"The Guttmanns have already lost one daughter [because she had not been able to return to Switzerland during the war] – don't make them lose another."

In St Margarethen, we were treated very well and looked after by a Swiss nurse. I remember Nurse Bianchi as a kindly spinster with neat hair that was always worn in a bun. She took a very benevolent interest in my welfare and used to buy me sweets as treats.

I was just ten years old at the time, and did not really understand why Nurse Bianchi went out of her way to care for us. I remember that my parents told her about our time in Bergen-Belsen and that she was utterly shocked by what had happened to us in the camps. This was the first she had heard of the full extent of the atrocities committed by the Nazis. It seems totally unbelievable to think that she was only a few kilometres from the German border and yet had spent the war in blissful ignorance of the wartime activities of the neighbouring country.

Later on, when we left St Margarethen, Nurse Bianchi remained in contact with my parents. She was very concerned about our well-being and even put us in contact with her brother and sister-in-law, who lived in Zürich and became our friends.

✡ ✡ ✡

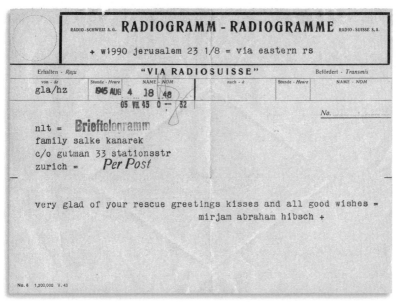

Telegram sent to my parents in Zürich by my uncle and aunt, Abraham and Mirjam Hirsch, Palestine, August 1945

My grandparents' apartment block in Zürich

ZÜRICH 1945–6

We were finally permitted to join my grandparents in Zürich in the summer of 1945. We knew that this, too, would be a temporary move. At the time, my father was in no condition to work, but even if he had been fit enough, my parents were under no illusions. They knew that even if they had wanted to remain in Switzerland, the authorities would not have allowed this.

It must have been something of a bitter-sweet reunion for my family. We were all painfully aware of the loss of my aunt and uncle, Miri and Yechiel Erdman. Although this was not discussed openly when I was around, it must have caused my grandparents immense grief, particularly since they had tried in vain to arrange for their release from Drancy and felt totally helpless in their efforts to save them from deportation.

By this time, I was ten years old and my grandparents' apartment seemed to me to be totally different from the place I had visited during holidays and festivals before the war. Over the four years in which I hadn't seen my grandparents, I felt that everything had changed. When we first returned to Zürich, I felt so sure that I had remembered their home in accurate detail, but somehow when I saw it all again, I was surprised to find that the mental picture I had kept in my head bore little similarity to reality. For some reason, I was very disturbed by the fact that my recollection was so inaccurate. It was probably this confused feeling about what was real and what was imagined that made me unwilling to talk about my time in the camps. I felt that the strangeness of my childhood experiences, combined with so much illness and upheaval, had played tricks on my memory.

My grandparents seemed older, and the constant anguish that my grandmother had suffered during the war had taken a heavy toll on her health. She suffered from high blood pressure and diabetes, yet she still worked hard as a sales representative and was actively travelling and selling garments in the villages outside Zürich.

My grandparents were incredibly warm and kind-hearted people, but although it was good to be in a normal environment after years of camp life, we were still not in our own home and there was a temporary feeling to life in Zürich. The fact that we were all still undergoing medical treatment made me feel quite unsettled.

I was still having regular injections for my severe frostbite and I was also sent to recuperate to various children's homes situated near Lake Constance. I also attended school in Zürich where I made a few friends and the teacher, Fräulein Kremer, took a benevolent interest in my welfare and school work. But my school life was interrupted regularly by bouts of illness and medical appointments.

During this time, clothes and medical care were provided by a Swiss Jewish charity for refugees, and although I am sure that my parents were grateful for the help we received, our reduced circumstances must have been distressing for everyone.

Zahava at school in Zürich, third row, far left

I remember that I used to have a few girl friends from the local Jewish community and they would come round on *Shabbat* afternoons to play. This was the beginning of rebuilding the normal childhood that I had totally missed out on in preceding years.

My grandparents were very good company and I enjoyed listening to humorous Jewish folk stories that my grandmother told me. She had the ability to keep me and my friends amused for hours.

My grandfather had a wonderful singing voice and we would sing *Zemirot*, festive songs during the *Shabbat* meals with him. It was comforting to begin to recreate family life together. But because we didn't have Jehudi with us yet, my parents could not feel entirely happy.

On 23 July 1945, my parents sent a telegram to Annie Roodenburg, asking about Jehudi's well-being. They received a reply on 3 August and also a week later, they received a telegram from my father's friend and employer, Haskel Rubin, which also confirmed the fact that Jehudi was in good health.

Telegrams about Jehudi, summer 1945

My father made a slow and incomplete recovery after the war and was in and out of hospital for much of the time in 1945. However, by July 1945, it is evident that he was attempting to re-establish business contacts and find out what remained for us in Holland.

As the letter below indicates, there was no possibility of returning to our previous apartment. Like thousands of survivors, we had been made homeless and destitute by the war.

1 August 1945

Dear Kanarek family,

First of all, warmest congratulations. We received your letter in good health and are very happy to learn that you have arrived in Switzerland. So far, you are the only ones from the whole street from whom we have received good news, but we hope that many more will follow.

Here in Amsterdam, we have also had a terrible time, but you had far worse to endure, so I will spare you the details. One thing I have to let you know. Your apartment has been re-let and there is nothing left – but really nothing of your furniture and possessions – and that must be a terrible tragedy for you as there is nothing to be bought here – only on the black market. If you have to start again to set up home as it was before the war, then you need thousands and thousands of guilders. You just can't imagine the prices of today. I am writing all these things not to give you worries or difficulties, or to make your worries any greater. On the contrary, I only thought that perhaps you would be able to buy these things in Switzerland and then perhaps transport them to Holland.

If you think I can do anything for you here, please do write to me and I will do it as far as is possible for me. Now dear friends, as I have no further news, I will finish with warmest regards and again congratulations that you got out with the whole family.

The Jelles family

Hope to see you soon.

Fortunately, my father had kept some stock from his rainwear business, which he had deposited with his colleagues in different parts of Holland in 1942. Being a man of great foresight, he must have reasoned that by dividing his possessions, he would increase the likelihood of retrieving at least a proportion of the things he had left behind before the war. Luckily, most of his stock was kept for us by true friends. In spite of the terrible shortages during the war, my father's colleagues proved themselves to be honest. Although they had witnessed the mass deportations of the Jews, our friends had remained optimistic about the prospect of our return to Holland after the war.

There was a famine in Holland in 1944 and thousands died of starvation, yet the two letters below show that despite the tremendous hardships that they had suffered, these family friends had made great efforts to safeguard our property although they could easily have sold or exchanged it for food or money to help provide for their families. Mr Homan, the writer of letter below, did actually pay my father for the coats he sold, and we have a letter that documents this.

6 August 1945
Leeuwarden

Dear Family,

We received your letter with great happiness, from which we learned that you and your loved ones came through. On behalf of my wife and children, our sincerest congratulations and we hope to see you soon in good health in Leeuwarden.

We are, thank goodness, fine, though we were very anxious because of all the raids, but still got through it.

I had to take your goods out of the house a few times, because we were so worried that they would be discovered. One evening, I opened the chest with the coats, rolled them in rugs and gave them to friends. The other goods we have in the wardrobe, so that they appeared to be our own personal property. The coats we kept in the attic have not improved. Using my discretion, I sold some to good friends, but have not yet let them pay as I didn't know how much they cost. I thought that this was the right thing to do as they could not have been used any more. When you come back, you will let me know the price. I thought it better to deal with it in this manner. I have kept the other [coats] which are still alright. All your personal belongings are in good condition and I hope you will soon be able to use them in your own home.

When you come to Leeuwarden, I would like to be informed in advance so that we can get everything ready. We will be on holiday for the first week of September.

You will have to tell us quite a lot about all the atrocities you experienced, but thankfully, you are here to tell us about it. Many of your co-religionists have not come back. Thankfully, everything here is alright. Our family has grown since you were away – five children. Our little girl who was lying in plaster is now fine again.

Dear Kanarek family, I will finish, hoping that you receive this letter in good health and will soon return to Holland, move into your own home and spend many happy years, and that you will forget all the afflictions you have endured.

Meanwhile, warmest regards,

Mr and Mrs A J Homan and children

It is evident from the letters below that in the aftermath of the war, ordinary Dutch people were fully aware that most of the Dutch Jewish community had been murdered by the Nazis.

Leeuwarden, Friesland
7 August 1945

Dear Mr Kanarek and family,

First of all sincerest congratulations that you have all come through and in health, that you were able to escape the devil's clutches. The fact that you were able to escape is a miracle. There won't be many people who have managed to get the whole family out of the murderers' hands. My wife, of course, also sends her warmest congratulations.

We are all well. They also had me in their hands three times, but I was lucky to be able to get out of it. When we meet in person, we'll have quite a lot to chat about. Luckily (unluckily!), there will be plenty of time for that because there is nothing to do yet in business. There are few raw materials available, and if I were you I would try to stay in Switzerland for some time. Just try to get well all of you. How fortunate you must feel!

Your goods are all in first-class condition. Fortunately, when you come back you won't be completely without anything because at the moment there is such a lack of textiles. There is a terrible shortage. It was very clever of you and we were happy to be able to help you a little, in order to lessen the difficulties a bit.

Last week I spoke to Benjamin from Groningen – he was also in Bergen-Belsen – but he also luckily just got out in the nick of time; his wife and three children perished. What those Nazi barbarians have on their conscience – animals, that's what they are. Now, dear people, see you soon.

Best wishes,
Try to enjoy hospitable Switzerland,
Yours,
Wim Houwen

7 August 1945

Dear Mr and Mrs Kanarek,

I received your letter dated 7 July and was very happy to learn that you were able to survive the terrible events of the war and have arrived safely in Switzerland. I congratulate you with all my heart. To my deepest sorrow, our best friends were not so lucky and have all been murdered. You can imagine how sad we are about this.

We ourselves are, thankfully, healthy and have been able to survive the food shortages well. We also had very bad times – at the end [of the war] we had to live on 400 grams of bread and one kilogram of potatoes per person per week. That's why quite a lot of people in Amsterdam died of starvation. The situation is much better now, but the sorrow for our lost friends remains.

Let me know as soon as you are back in Amsterdam. In the meantime,

Best regards

Hoffels-Brun

Amsterdam

16 August 1945

Dear Kanarek family,

I received your letter of 12 July and was happy to learn that you escaped their clutches, even after a very great deal of misery.

Thankfully, we are all well and have reached the end of many difficult times.

I went to Amsterdam to collect the remains of your china, but it was just on the day that you were transported at night, so I do not know where the rest remains. I did not dare ask the seamstress, who lives above you, and I only hope that you will get it back.

I just hope that you regain your strength, and now that the war with Japan is over as well, that things will soon recover.

Warmest regards to you all,

D de Jong Ligtheart

The following letter from my father's friend and employer, Haskel Rubin, reveals in greater detail the extent to which our community had suffered during the war. The Rubins and their children, Fanny and Israel, stayed in hiding in Holland throughout the war. They had been instrumental in helping my parents make contact with the resistance in 1942 in order to hand over Jehudi, and had also kept in touch through Mrs Roodenburg. In his letter, Mr Rubin refers to our mutual friends who managed to survive. Although he does not state the fact explicitly, by then my parents were probably painfully aware of the reality – that the vast majority of our friends had perished.

Mr Rubin also writes with optimism about how quickly survivors were able to pick up the pieces of their previous existence and rebuild their lives. I think that to the outside world this might have seemed to be the case. Considering what they had endured in the war years, most of the survivors made a remarkably quick recovery in terms of finding work and settling back into the community.

I believe that when Mr Rubin wrote below that people were "well again amazingly soon", this was what people wanted to believe and this is how it appeared on the surface. However, for all of us, it was only a partial recovery; the physical and emotional scars went very deep, but there was a kind of unspoken rule that people did not discuss the horrific events of the past. To spend any time analysing the nature of the tragedy we had suffered would have totally paralysed us. The only way of moving on was to focus on the present and prepare for the future. I think that for this reason, my father was extremely keen to return to Holland to find employment and re-establish himself. However, of the three of us, my father's physical well-being had been affected most by his time in the concentration camps and for the rest of his life, he suffered from the after-effects.

23 August 1945

Dear Kanarek Family,

Today we received your letter, with which we were very happy. We have not received the registered letter that you mentioned, but we have received an ordinary letter. Here in Amsterdam, everything has changed a lot. Of the many acquaintances from before the war, unfortunately only very few have returned. The whole Jewish quarter has been demolished and during the last winter people had no gas and no coal, so they tore down the uninhabited houses to use the wood.

Of our friends, for example, those remaining here are the Feiwell family, Berger, Kleinberger with two daughters and a son of Chazan [Cantor] Maroko and a daughter of Chazan De Jong. Her mother and one brother have returned from Bergen-Belsen. Also the Szmul family, Hannah Rosenthal family and two daughters of the Shander family of the N. Prinsengracht, the Neuwirth family and Rav Bayer. So you can roughly imagine who is still here. Also the daughter of the Kanareks from Weesp has returned.

We ourselves are fine. In the meantime, the children have grown a lot. We are in our house again. Nothing remains of our old furniture. The Germans have stolen everything. In spite of this, we have been able to refurnish a bit. The workshop is functional again so we can begin to work, although many machines were stolen. After the capitulation, there was great chaos. Gradually, the economic situation is getting a bit better, very slowly. Koppel Birnhak is back in Amsterdam with his wife, but he himself is very sick, having been in Bergen-Belsen. He fell ill and then got pleurisy. Yesterday, his condition improved a bit. As you wrote, your wife did not return in very good health. After all the difficulties that you experienced there, that is certainly not surprising.

I hope that when she finally returns to Holland, she will have fully recovered. Most people who have come back from the camps are well again amazingly soon once they are in normal circumstances. We are happy to hear that Zahavi is now such a big girl and hopefully we will meet again soon in Holland. I can just imagine how much you are longing to see your child. There is no further news to write.

Warmest greetings,

Haskel Rubin

PS Your boy has grown a lot. He's not blonde any more and is now quite dark. Fanny is going to visit him next week.

132

The following letter is of interest because it stands out among all the letters received from my father's acquaintances. It again reveals the desperate struggle of Dutch people during and after the war. Although the writer is aware that my parents have just emerged from the concentration camps, he is hopeful that they might have contacts to help him find work in Switzerland!

I can actually recall my parents discussing this man, who was only able to keep the *machzorim*, the festival prayer books that my parents had entrusted to him. All the other items they had handed to him for safe-keeping had somehow met a mysterious fate and were not to be found after the war. My parents had laughed about the irony of the situation. Obviously, Hebrew prayer books had little value on the black market in Nazi-occupied Holland! Despite the fact that everything we had given this man had been taken, I remember that my mother was very happy that the *machzorim* had been preserved for her during the war. They were an engagement gift from my paternal grandparents – and now the only memento she had of them. Later, we learned that my father's parents were among the millions who had perished in Auschwitz.

Amsterdam
12 September 1945

Dear Kanarek Family,
With great joy, we learnt from your letter that you have arrived safely in Switzerland. We hope that both your children are also well, as you did not mention anything about them in your letter.
We can understand that you had to suffer greatly in Bergen-Belsen – particularly as I had to spend some time in prison, because of hiding an American pilot for about two years.
I was betrayed due to an unfortunate event and a large part of my

possessions fell into the hands of the Germans and were confiscated. My life hung on a silk thread and I was only lucky because they had to leave suddenly. All of us, including my wife and daughter, suffered from hunger and if it had lasted a little longer, we would all have died of starvation.

We are all happy that the war is over. I will tell you more when you come back, but for the moment you should try to stay in Switzerland if you can. About 15,000 flats were destroyed; one cannot earn anything and money has to be reorganised. I myself have no job and problems getting necessities. Are there any companies in Switzerland looking for representatives in Holland? It does not have to be in the car industry.

I was able to keep your prayer books and hide them from the Germans, so you can have these back at any time.

The reason I did not answer you earlier was that I was in Groningen to regain my strength. But as soon as I returned to Amsterdam, I wanted to reply immediately.

I hope you receive this letter in the best of health. Now you have heard something from Holland and I will finish with kindest regards to you, your wife and children, and also from my wife and daughter.

Greetings,

Petr Linden

The following letter was actually sent with an enclosed photograph, showing the extent of devastation following the bombing of the town of Groningen. It makes pitiful reading, since the writer was made homeless by the bombing, another of the thousands of innocent people who lost everything during the war.

Photograph enclosed in Mr Jansen's letter (opposite), showing the remains of his premises after the bombing in Groningen

Groningen
24 September 1945

Dear Mr Kanarek,
I received both your letters and thank you for them. Your first letter
arrived almost at the same time as your second, the reason being that I
could not be found in Groningen.

When the town was liberated, Groningen was severely damaged. The
whole town centre is a heap of rubble. Grote Markt and the north side,
where we used to live, are completely destroyed, as well as the east and
west sides. Also the WaagStraat, Juldenstraat and part of Ebbingestraat.
The Meyering Company on the Fishmarket also no longer exists.
Because our house and shop burnt down, I stayed at the homes of various
family members and had no fixed address. For the last few weeks, we
have been at temporary premises with another firm. The premises are
far too small, but for the time being, we have to manage. I am sorry to
tell you that your cases were also lost in the fire. Only a lady's watch
and a brooch, which I kept in the safe, were saved. I enclose a photo of
the premises: these are the remains days after the fire. Now there isn't a
stone left and the whole market has been cleared on three sides. It will
take quite some time before we get the premises at Grotemarkt back.

A fortnight ago, I was in Amsterdam with Messrs Weinstock. The
family is well. Mr Weinstock told me that you are already in Switzerland
but will return to Holland soon.

I hope to see you soon and we will be able to tell each other about our
tribulations.

With warmest regards,
R Jansen

We do not have any further correspondence from my father's
colleagues after this, but this is probably because in the autumn of
1945, he was actively making plans to return to Amsterdam.

Although colleagues advised him against returning to Holland
too soon after the war, my father wanted very much to go back.

After five years when the possibility of earning a living had been denied him, he was keen to start working again. His forward planning had meant that he still had a significant amount of stock from before the war, so he actually had something to sell. As there was a great shortage of textiles in Europe, he reasoned that once he had recovered his strength, he would be in a relatively fortunate position. In November 1945, although he had not fully recovered, he was well enough to travel to Holland and try to start to prepare for our return there.

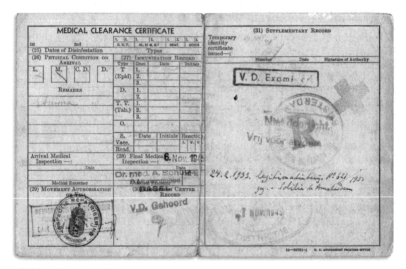

Salke's medical card, 1945

Looking back on our time in Zürich, it is now clear that I was in Switzerland with my mother for over a year, from the summer of 1945 onwards. But since this time was punctuated with hospital visits and lengthy periods of recuperation, I don't remember it feeling like a settled period in my life.

Salke's repatriation card, 1945

It must have been distressing for my mother to be apart from her young son for a full year after the war ended, but clearly she had no choice. We were effectively homeless and neither of my parents was physically well enough to care for Jehudi.

After the famine in Holland, when many children died of starvation, Jehudi had been fortunate and was among those sent to Copenhagen by the Red Cross. After this, he was cared for by my mother's cousin, Regina (Rex) Hermann, in Stockholm. As we can see from the letter below, in January 1946 he was still suffering from the effects of malnutrition.

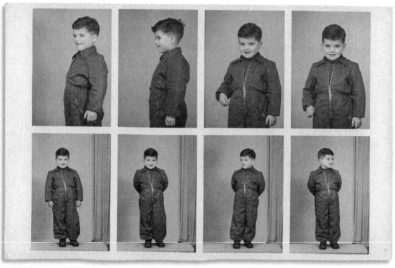

Jehudi, aged four

Stockholm
8 January 1946

My Dear Rosy,
How do you like your little darling? He was not at all cooperative at first [to pose for the photographer] as he is very preoccupied with his little bike from early morning till nightfall. I had great difficulty in persuading him to come to the photographer as he was. This has the advantage of looking more natural than when you dress them up for that purpose.

*He is very well and you should see how happy the little chap is, and
how many friends he has made. Tomorrow, I have to take him to the
doctor again regarding his gut...*

*I am waiting for your agreement and then he should be operated on
immediately. Don't worry about anything as he is in the best care, and
actually it's not dangerous.*

Hope to hear from you soon,

Lots of love,

Rex

A week later, Regina wrote to my mother again, this time telling
her that Jehudi had been admitted to hospital with persistent
digestive problems.

Stockholm

14 January 1946

Dear Rosy

*On Wednesday, after the doctor's examination, Jultje was immediately
admitted to the hospital, because the doctor said it could be dangerous if
he walked about any longer like this.*

*For the time being, he is on a diet and under observation when he
strains...*

*If the situation doesn't get better, he will have to be operated on. He
is in the best of care in the Children's Hospital and, as I saw for myself
yesterday, he feels comfortable there. All the children lie in big glass boxes
and Jultje finds this very funny. This time he went to the hospital
without protesting. When I told him that he had to stay there, he cried
a lot, but when I promised I would continue to be his Mummy and visit
him often, he became very quiet and followed the nurse. Nurse Birgitta
told me yesterday that he is very adaptable and easy to take care of. I
bought him a [toy] telephone that he had wanted for a long time. He
immediately phoned all our children and friends, and then he phoned
you. He said, "Hello Mummy in Switzerland, I am a good boy and*

don't cry, but they don't give me any meat (meat is his favourite) and soon I'll come home with Mami, Papi, Gerhard, Renata and Rainer [Regina's family]."

I was very surprised that he spoke to you, because when I've spoken about you, he has always answered that you are not his Mummy.

By the way Jultje is not at all over-sensitive. On the contrary, he is a brave little boy... He is very attached to me and difficult when I'm not at home only because he is frightened that I won't return. You can see clearly that he has felt very vulnerable at times and has suffered a great deal. I have often thought that for you, the very worst thing must have been that Zahavi has been deprived so much and to see her suffer so much. That must surely have made her grow up much faster and it must have made her more serious. If you have a photo of her, think of me. Jultje looks incredibly like you, particularly the way he presents himself and his movements. I wish you were here. Sigmund wrote that he will come to Sweden as soon as he gets the papers to have his operation. Is it a major operation? At least you will have him there [with you in Switzerland]. Conditions in Holland will return to normality quicker than we first thought. One can see this in the case of Norway which suffered so much. Conditions have improved to some extent, not to mention Denmark. How are your dear parents?

Regina Hermann

At the time when Regina wrote this letter, Jehudi was not yet five years old, but having lived in so many homes and been cared for by a variety of different people, his confusion about the identity of his mother is totally understandable.

Regina also reflects on the psychological trauma that we had all endured living as a fragmented family. I think that for my parents, it must have been tremendously difficult being separated from their son, then emerging from the war, knowing that he would have no recollection of them.

As for me, I was a child and although I remembered Jehudi as an adorable baby, I had been 'an only child' for so long that I didn't actively miss my younger brother. I was just acutely aware of his absence and of the sadness that the separation caused my parents.

My father returned to Holland again in early November 1945 and this was the first stage in preparing for our return. Like most of the Jewish refugees, he no longer had a home to which he could return and so he stayed in the *Joodsche Invalide*. The history of the *Joodsche Invalide* reflects the history of the Dutch community.

Before the war, it had been the Jewish care home for the physically handicapped. It was renowned for giving its residents the most innovative treatments and made the lives of those who lived there as meaningful as possible. In the 1930s it outgrew its premises and money was raised to establish a state-of-the-art building funded by donors from both the Jewish and non-Jewish communities of Amsterdam. This new building was opened in 1937 and there was a well-documented visit by Princess Juliana in 1938. The care home accommodated 400 residents as well as a large and dedicated staff. On 1 March 1943, the Nazis 'emptied' the *Joodsche Invalide* and all residents and staff were deported.

By the middle of 1945, there was no longer a need for a care home for the physically handicapped in Amsterdam. The *Joodsche Invalide* was hastily converted to a centre where survivors and displaced people could stay. It was a place from which people could try to trace their missing relatives and it served as a temporary base for those like my father who had lost their homes. My father's main concern at this time was to see Jehudi and organise a home for our return to Amsterdam.

Since my parents had no money, the costs of both my father's travel and medical care had to be covered. My mother kept many of the documents from the time. These show that the costs were met both by Jewish charities and the Dutch Ministry of Social Affairs.

My father was still unwell and in need of an operation. In this testimonial below, my grandmother writes to the Swiss Immigration Office, asking permission for him to travel to Switzerland for surgery.

Correspondence seeking charitable help, 1945

Testimonial from Rifka Guttman concerning Sigmund Kanarek sent to the Immigration Office in Switzerland

5 March 1946

I request permission for my son-in-law, Salke Kanarek, to travel to Switzerland. He is now in Holland and his wife, my daughter, and their little girl are still in Switzerland. I would like my son-in-law to travel for health reasons. He was sent from Holland to Bergen-Belsen, where he was in a concentration camp... He was sick when he arrived in Switzerland, but left on 6 November 1945 to find his little son. He was already ill when he was in Switzerland and under medical treatment, yet he rushed back to Holland to prepare for the arrival of his wife and children. Now, unfortunately, his condition has deteriorated greatly and he has to have an operation immediately. This cannot take place in Holland as it is partially destroyed. Besides, in Switzerland, there is a precedent for performing this operation and it is known throughout the world for this.

My son-in-law requires this operation urgently, but before it can be done, the inflammation of the jaw must settle. All these problems originate from Bergen-Belsen. The operation must be done in such a way that it does not result in any complications. This is why we have to think of a stay of five or six weeks. After his recovery, he would like to take his wife and young daughter to Holland. As his wife has not yet fully recovered, she is unable to undertake the journey at present. I am requesting, therefore, that you grant permission for my son-in-law's stay in Zürich from the beginning of April until the middle of May this year. He has the means to cover all the costs. Also, he is not in need of an apartment because he will be staying with me, both before and after the operation. I enclose herewith the doctor's certificate.

The operation to which my grandmother refers was thyroid surgery (for a goitre). This was due to the starvation diet on which my father had subsisted in Bergen-Belsen, which had left him very weak. I remember that he had persistent thyroid problems, but I don't know whether the Swiss authorities granted him permission to have the operation there. The documents show that he was in Holland in early April 1946 so he did not have the operation immediately, as my grandmother had requested.

At around the same time, I was sent on my first big trip alone. I was ten years old at the time. I was to travel by train to a children's home in Wattwil in the Swiss mountains. This was one of the many efforts that my parents made to aid my recuperation. I don't think my mother was happy to send me away on my own, but since my father was travelling to and from Holland and was awaiting an operation, and my mother was still a hospital out-patient, she probably felt that she had little choice. She also very much wanted me to be with other children again.

Some of the cost of the third-class train fare was paid for by the Swiss authorities. The day after I left my mother wrote to me:

8 March 1946

My Very Dear Zahavi,

Last night I came in and I had just missed your call by ten minutes. What a pity! I would so much have liked to hear your voice, but nothing could be done about it.

You know, my dearest, Mummy has to go to the hospital in the afternoon and after that I had to get a few things.

Dear Zahavi, how was your first trip alone? Did the conductor help you to take your suitcase to the other train? Did Mrs Kremer collect you from the train at Wattwil? I was so glad that you arrived on time.

Last night Alice Mohl came to visit me and she brought some biscuits for you. I'll send them to you next week. I am writing this card from the waiting room at hospital.

I hope that when I next hear from you, you will tell me how everything is. I hope you have the chance to go tobogganing. That would be wonderful. I am sure that after such a long journey you must have slept well. Are there many children there? Have you found a friend yet? If you need anything, let me know immediately. Eat an orange every day! Don't let them go bad.

I wish you a very good shabbos *[Sabbath] and send you many kisses. I hope you have a good holiday,*
Mami
Extra kisses from Opa and Oma

This letter really shows my mother as she was – she expresses all her maternal concerns and is overwhelmingly loving and protective. This trip, which must have been a few weeks' long, was to provide me with mountain air and companionship. My mother had even given me a supply of oranges to help boost my immune system after we had been deficient in vitamin C for so long!

My mother wrote to me regularly when I was away and the following letter from around the same time is further evidence of her affection. Also, although we still had not been reunited with Jehudi, my mother was keen to remind me of him and thoughtfully enclosed a photograph of him.

> *Dear Zahavi,*
>
> *Unfortunately I came home so late on Friday from the hospital that I was unable to send you this card before* Shabbos. *All* Shabbos, *I was upset about this as I knew, my darling, that you were waiting for your* Shabbos *letter. That's why you will get a double lot to read on Monday.*
>
> *I didn't receive any post from Daddy again today. Opa was upset that you didn't add greetings to him. In future, don't forget to do that! Just have plenty of rest. For today, I'll end with thousands of kisses,*
> *Your Mami*
> *Special regards to Mrs Kremer and Mrs Wolf.*
> *And, dearest darling, we also send you many greetings and kisses,*
> *Oma and Opa*
> *PS I enclose a small picture of Jehudi*

It seems that during 1946 we were a very fragmented family. The letter below shows that I also spent some time in a children's home in Heiden, while my mother was in Zürich, my father in Amsterdam and my brother in Stockholm. It is hardly surprising that in the short letter below, I am slightly concerned about the welfare of the other members of my family. I think that these extended trips for my convalescence, when I was separated from my parents, were endured rather than enjoyed!

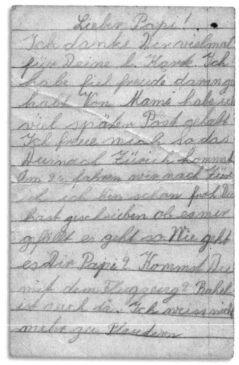

Zahava's letter to her father, 1946

Heiden
15 July 1946

Dear Daddy,

    Many thanks for your card. I was very happy with it. I received a letter from Mummy, much later.

    I am very pleased that you are coming to Zürich. On 24th we are going to Zürich. You asked whether I like it here. It is alright. How are you, darling Daddy? Are you coming by plane? Rachel is also here.

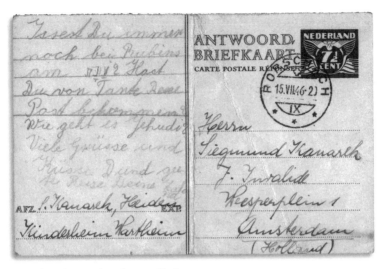

I don't know what else to talk about.

Are you still eating at the Rubins on Shabbos? *Have you had any post from Auntie Rex? How is Jehudi?*

Lots of love and kisses,

Have a safe journey.

Yours, Zahava

It seems that after my father visited us in Zürich in summer 1946, he returned to Amsterdam in the autumn and made permanent plans for our return there. I do not recall whether we were together for *Rosh Hashanah*, (the Jewish New Year), but my mother and I would have been in Zürich for the high Holydays. There must have been some reason why my father was in Amsterdam during the subsequent festival of *Succot*, (Tabernacles) because we have a receipt showing that he had his meals and stayed at the *Joodsche Invalide* at that time.

He would not have chosen to be apart from us during the festival period. I think he must have needed to stay in Amsterdam in order to register our family for a new home. The note opposite, written the day before the start of *Succot*, shows that I was registered at our new home in Amsterdam from that date, although we did not actually move into our apartment in Katwijkstraat until the end of November 1946.

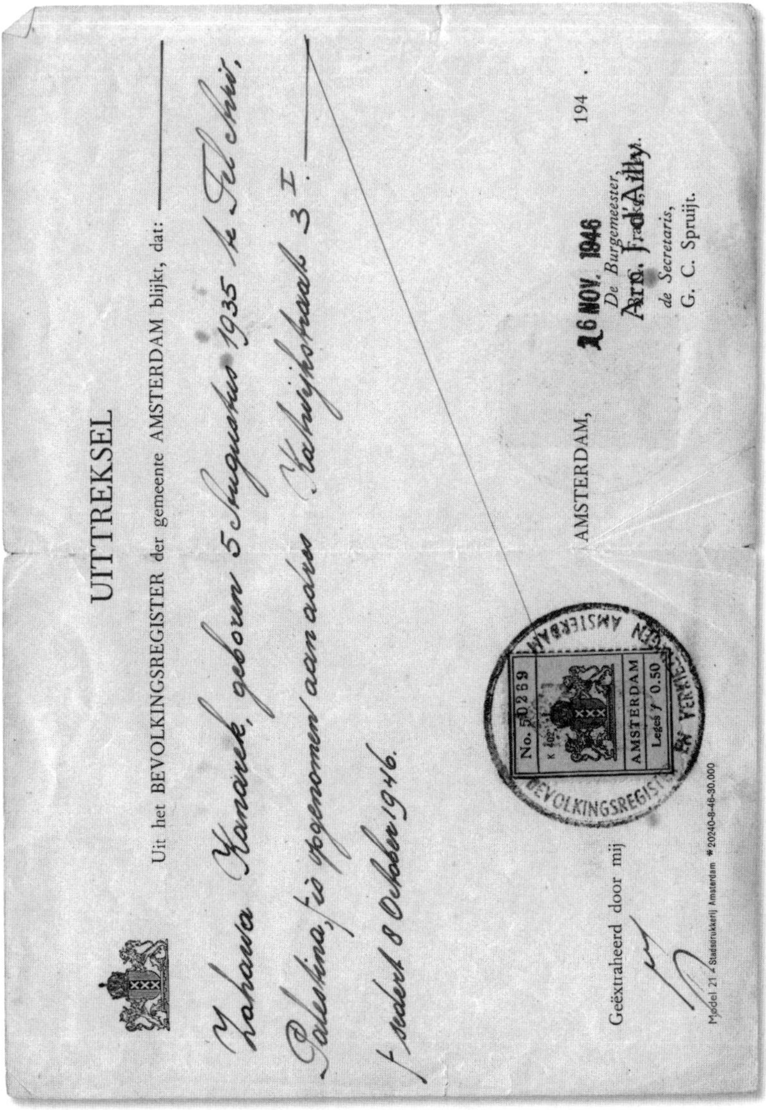

UITTREKSEL

Uit het BEVOLKINGSREGISTER der gemeente AMSTERDAM blijkt, dat:

Zahawa Kanarek, geboren 5 Augustus 1935 te Tel Aviv.

Palestina, is opgenomen aan adres Valerijkstraat 3.

I. nederk 8 Oktober 1946.

Geëxtraheerd door mij

Middel 21 • Stadsdrukkerij Amsterdam * 20240-8-46-50.000

AMSTERDAM, **16 NOV. 1946** 194

De Burgemeester,
Arn. Fred. Althy.

de Secretaris,
G. C. Spruijt.

No. 50259

K 402

AMSTERDAM
XXX
Leges ƒ 0.50

BEVOLKINGSREGIS...

Extract from Amsterdam Register, showing our new address

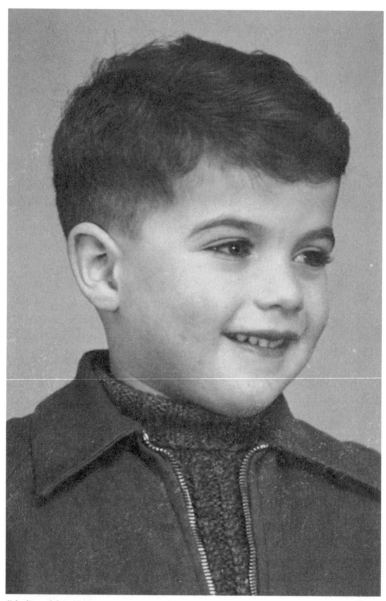

Jehudi, aged five, 1946

JEHUDI

While we had been struggling to survive in the camps, Jehudi was a small child living a parallel existence in Nazi-occupied Holland. He was just a tiny child when he was separated from us and we remained apart for three and a half years. Curiously, Jehudi has no memory of the war period. He attributes this total amnesia to the fact that those early years were difficult for him, both physically and psychologically. Later, the war and events connected with it were never discussed in our home. Although Jehudi has excellent recall of the time after the war, he believes that this complete block was a form of self-preservation. What follows is the broad outline of events as they were told to him afterwards.

Jehudi was just over one year old when he was handed to the Resistance and then placed in an orphanage in Heemstede, between Haarlem and Amsterdam. There were 45 children in the orphanage with him. It is likely that he was among other Jewish children whose parents had sought desperately to find a means of saving their children by placing them in the care of others.

One day, probably early in 1943, the Gestapo came to 'inspect' the orphanage. In customary fashion, they scrutinised all the children there. They then seized 43 of the children and took them away. They were convinced that these were all Jewish children and consequently sent them to their deaths in Auschwitz. Only two children remained. Having looked closely at these babies for their Jewish features, they were sure that Jehudi, with his blonde hair and blue eyes, could not be Jewish. So because of his Aryan features, my brother's life was spared.

After that, since the Nazis had obliterated the need for the orphanage, another home had to be found for Jehudi. Fortunately, the Dutch Resistance took him and placed him in the care of a lady who was to be his guardian for the duration of the war. Jehudi was looked after by Nurse Stol from 20 February 1943 until May 1945.

Nurse Stol was a Dutch Protestant with a family of her own. In the difficult years of the war she was very short of money and in need of a salary to provide for her family and so she was paid to look after Jehudi. She had several people in her care as well as four of her own children; altogether there were ten people living in her house.

On one occasion, Nurse Stol took Jehudi to have his hair cut. The Dutch barber asked her who Jehudi was. He then looked at him and said, "I could swear that's a Jewish boy." Nurse Stol said nothing, but she was very frightened. From that time on, it was decided that it would be safer to keep Jehudi indoors as much as possible.

There was also another incident when, as a little boy, Jehudi ran outside into the garden not wearing any trousers. Nurse Stol was in shock and made him come back to her and stand in her porch. She then picked him up and carried him in such a way that evidence of his Jewish identity was not on view! There was an office of the NSB (*Nationaal-Socialistische Beweging*, the Dutch Nazi party) next door to the Stols' house. Even as a tiny child, Jehudi was made aware that revealing his true religion would put his adopted family in grave danger.

In the winter of 1944, when Jehudi was three years old, he needed an intestinal operation. This had to be done in secret with the help of the Resistance, and the surgery took place in Haarlem. Obviously, the prospect of organising an operation on a circumcised child in Nazi-occupied Holland was risky. Had this procedure been discovered, all those involved would have been implicated and the Nazis were known to be particularly brutal with people who helped Jews.

Fortunately, the operation was carried out successfully and was never discovered, but Jehudi had further problems with his health. In 1944, the devastation caused by the Dutch famine killed much of the civilian population. Like many young children, Jehudi suffered from malnutrition – he had a swollen belly, having been fed tulip bulbs because there was little else for him to eat. As a result, in the summer of 1945, Jehudi was among a group of children taken from Holland to Copenhagen by the Red Cross.

The Stol children were very upset when Jehudi was to leave their family; they felt he was like a brother to them. When he was collected by a Red Cross representative, one of the children remembers crying. They were all worried that if someone came to collect Jehudi, perhaps later someone else would come for them.

It is not clear how long Jehudi stayed in Copenhagen, but he was probably there during the summer and autumn of 1945. After that,

Regina Hermann, Rosy's cousin went to collect him and took him to join her family in Stockholm. Jehudi lived with her for about a year until November 1946, when we went to Sweden to bring him home.

Jehudi grew up with Regina's three children in Stockholm. The family lived on Stramalivegan16, Bromma, near the airport. Jehudi became friendly with the people who worked there and even earned some money doing small jobs for them. He was five at the time. Ironically, they named him *Jesus child* on account of his blonde hair and Aryan features.

In the autumn of 1946, after we had recuperated enough to travel, my mother and I made the journey to Stockholm to be reunited with Jehudi. The journey was very exciting for me because it was rare to travel by plane in those days. As the plane swooped in to land, we seemed to go dangerously close to the sea. I screamed out, "Did we survive Bergen-Belsen only to be killed here?" This was something heard by other passengers and it was remembered for a long time afterwards. I was 11 at the time.

During our time in the camps, we knew little of what was happening to Jehudi. In fact, in order to be safe, we were unable to speak about him openly. I knew I had a brother, but we had been apart for so long and suffered so much that I can't remember feeling emotionally involved with this child whom I had last seen when he was a baby. Now Jehudi was a little boy who spoke Swedish. I was told that he was my brother, but the process of becoming reacquainted with one another must have been very awkward for everyone, and particularly difficult for my mother. She wanted the transition period for Jehudi to be gradual, to ease the trauma for him.

I remember the children in Stockholm teaching me Swedish songs and I enjoyed the company of Regina Hermann's children, but bonding with my newly-found brother was to be a slow process.

We stayed in Sweden for some weeks and wanted Jehudi to get used to being with us and weaned off his attachment to Regina. He must have felt very confused, particularly since by that time he was fluent in Swedish and we spoke Dutch to him. He already felt that he had had two mothers – Nurse Stol and then Regina Hermann. Now a strange lady had come from Switzerland, claiming to be his real mother. He referred to our mother as the *Die Mutti aus der Schweiz*.

My mother told us that they tried many different means to persuade him to come back with us. We bought him several gifts, among which was a large balloon to which he became very attached. Gradually, over a period of days, the balloon deflated. We told him that Daddy in Holland would be able to give him many more balloons and would also be able to inflate the deflated balloon. After that, my mother told us that, "Jehudi couldn't wait to go back to Amsterdam with us and kept asking when we would be going there." When my mother felt we had bonded sufficiently, we travelled back to Holland with him.

Only recently, we found this letter which shows that my mother fell ill while we were in Stockholm and that Rex had wanted my father to come and take us back since Jehudi was quite a handful! The letter implies that it would have been a struggle for my mother to travel with us on her own. In the event, I believe she did manage to take us both back to Holland, although this could not have been easy. Yet in subsequent years, the difficulties of that period were never discussed.

Stockholm
13 November 1946

Dear Sigmund,

   Unfortunately, I have to write to let you know that your dear wife is feeling very poorly. The journey here has affected her very badly and she is worried about travelling back with the two children.

   As Rosy wants to return home as soon as possible, I wonder if you could possibly come here to fetch her? She will feel much better in her own home. Here, she rests for most of the day and I can't imagine her being able to make the journey on her own.

   Could you possibly make it here next week? It's best to send me a telegram. I'm sure you will be happy to have your whole family home.

   I await your speedy reply and send you regards and kisses,
Yours,
Cousin Regina Hermann
PS Jehudi has to be taken back by force and will need an adult who is able to take care of him, and so Rosy will have difficulty looking after both the children.

Jehudi in Holland, summer 1945

Zahava, with long plaits, and Jehudi outside 3 Katwijkstraat, Amsterdam

REBUILDING SHATTERED LIVES
1946–51

The Amsterdam to which we returned after the Holocaust bore little resemblance to the vibrant town that had existed prior to the Nazi occupation. Around 75 per cent of the Jewish population had been murdered.

Much of the Jewish area that had been the central focus of our life had been ransacked and destroyed. The fuel shortage of the previous winter had meant that the wood from which many of the homes were built had been taken and used as firewood. The few Jews who were able to return found that their homes were fully occupied and their personal possessions and furniture had been stolen or destroyed.

Yet in spite of hearing about this, my parents were very keen to return to their home town. At the end of 1946, my mother and I were finally well enough to join my father in the small flat in Amsterdam that we had been given by the Dutch Government. Both of my parents wanted very much to resume a normal life.

We were given a tiny first floor flat at 3 Katwijkstraat on the outskirts of Amsterdam. It consisted of a bedroom for my parents, a minute bedroom for my brother and me, a kitchen, toilet and shower. There was also a small dining room where my parents entertained guests and relatives who came to visit.

The flat had been occupied by the NSB, the Dutch Nazi party. I remember that we found food and some possessions in the apartment, but the very thought of having any contact with anything used by the Nazi occupants was so repellent to us that my parents threw away all the remnants.

The apartment had obviously been abandoned when it became clear that Germany would lose the war. The effect of the Dutch famine of 1944 lasted well into 1945, when there was widespread malnutrition and starvation, yet it was clear from the evidence left in the flat that Nazi sympathisers had always been well provided for and had never suffered the privations of the rest of society.

When we returned to Holland with Jehudi, we could finally begin life as a complete family. Although this must have been a huge period of readjustment for us all, I don't remember it as difficult or traumatic in any way. Indeed, the photos show that it was quite a happy time for our family.

We felt optimistic about the future. I had learnt some Swedish during our prolonged stay in Sweden and so was able to talk to Jehudi easily. He was an adaptable child and quick to learn new things, and so for all of us it was wonderful to be united.

Although our apartment was more modest than our previous home, my parents recreated the life that we had enjoyed prior to the war. Whenever possible, they invited guests and we often had to give up our tiny bedrooms for visitors from out of town.

Since we had missed so much in the way of education, we were both very happy to attend school. Jehudi and I both went to the Rosh Pinah School in Van Ostade Straat.

Zahava's class at Rosh Pinah School, 1947. Zahava is in the centre, on the teacher's left

This photo (p.162) shows me at the centre of my class next to our teacher, Mr van Saxen. He was a lovely man who taught us all the main secular subjects. The children on this photograph are a mixed bunch. The majority had been hidden in Holland during the war, but I know that one boy was in Indonesia during the war and a few lucky ones went to relatives in Switzerland. Some, like me, had been in concentration camps. We came from different religious backgrounds and our ages varied from around ten to thirteen. Despite our diverse backgrounds and experiences, we all had one thing in common – we had missed out on vital years of schooling, so Mr van Saxen's job must have been very challenging!

Every child in this photo had experienced his or her own individual trauma during the war and because of this shared history, we all became very close. There was the sense that despite everything, we had all managed to survive. Although we might have known about what had happened to our classmates and their families, there was an unspoken understanding that it was never discussed. I may not have been aware of this at the time, but I think that what we all wanted to create for ourselves was a sense of normality and security. Consequently, I don't ever remember talking to Jehudi about our experiences in Belsen, nor do I recall hearing about what he had experienced during his time with Nurse Stol.

My parents also wanted to compensate for the years in which we had received no religious education, so in addition to our normal school day, which ended around four in the afternoon, after school and on Sunday mornings, we attended a *Talmud Torah*. Here we gained a deeper understanding of our religion and the *Torah*. Our teacher, Mr Mundstuck, was very knowledgeable and today I still remember much of what he taught me. He had been hidden in Holland during the war. I very much enjoyed his lessons, partly because I was the only girl in my class at the time. Mr Mundstuck also gave private lessons to other students.

There were probably very few people in Holland after the war who were able to teach religious studies because so many scholars and rabbis had been killed. Later, I discovered that one of Mr Mundstuck's private students was my husband Ralph, although back in 1947, I was not even aware of his existence!

Photo of the HBS School, 1950. Zahava is seated next to the teacher, on the third row back, far left.

After Rosh Pinah, I had to sit the entrance exams for the Jewish Secondary School – the *Joodse Hoge Burger School*, known as HBS – which later became the Maimonides School.

Some other children from my primary school who passed the entrance test for the HBS are also with me in this photograph. Although I enjoyed my time there and remember cycling happily to and from school each day, I never felt that I could focus totally on my schoolwork during that period. This was because I was often needed to help at home as my father had persistent health problems.

In the years after the war, it seemed to me that life returned to normality with surprising ease. My parents found some old friends whom they had known before the war. For them, it must have been terribly difficult because the vast majority of the people they had known previously simply never returned. But I was only really made aware of how glad they were to be reunited with those who had come through. They also made new friends who would come to visit us.

Unlike our previous home in Amsterdam, our apartment was far away from synagogues and the Jewish centre of the city. During the week, this was not so much of a problem because we used the tram to get into town and people would travel to visit us. *Shabbat*, however, was more difficult since we would not use transport. My father and Jehudi would walk for the best part of an hour to get to the *shtiebl*. This was a small synagogue favoured by Jews who originated from Eastern Europe. Looking back on it, these walks must have provided them with the opportunity to make up for lost time and build up their relationship.

I didn't join them since I had always preferred cantorial music and favoured a more formal type of synagogue. The large *shul* which I chose to attend was only half an hour's walk away. My mother was not able to make the long walk with me. On *Rosh Hashanah* and *Yom Kippur*, our family would stay in the centre of town so that my mother could also attend synagogue.

For major festivals such as *Pesach* and *Succot*, we continued our tradition of joining my maternal grandparents in Zürich. My grandfather used to lead the services at the synagogue there. He had a beautiful singing voice, which we all enjoyed. We did this for many years because it enabled my mother to attend synagogue services, which was not feasible in Amsterdam.

The Kanarek family with grandparents Josef and Rivka Guttmann in Zürich

From a child's perspective, the whole emphasis in those years was on enjoying the present and planning for a better future. I am sure that my parents must have talked to each other about their experiences. But in their conversations with us, the past was not dwelt upon; in the main, we tried to forget about our negative experiences and, on reflection, I think we were successful. I always had many friends and became very involved in *Bnei Akiva*, the Zionist Youth Movement, and I used to walk into town on a *Shabbat* afternoon to be with my friends.

Fortunately, my father was able to resume his employment after the war with the Jewish-owned rainwear company that he had worked for previously. His employer, Mr Rubin, had been in hiding in Holland and had emerged after the war with his entire family.

In the difficult time following the Holocaust, many people from Europe were attempting to make their way to Palestine. The experience of the concentration camps had demonstrated to Jews everywhere that they would never be entirely safe or free until they had their own country. A large number of young people went to settle in Palestine and many young men went to fight in the war of independence in 1948. Sadly, there were a number of people who survived the camps only to be killed fighting for the State of Israel.

I remember that the Rubin family opened their house to a group of young camp survivors from Poland who were en route to Palestine. They covered the floor of their grand reception room with mattresses and gave hospitality to these young people, who would otherwise have been homeless.

These few Polish Jewish survivors had tried to return to post-war Poland and had been greeted with violence – the Poles who had seized the Jews' property when they were deported were terrified that they would come and reclaim what was rightfully theirs. After the war, pogroms in Poland were commonplace and a number of survivors were killed by Polish mobs. So the Polish Jewish survivors were among the most desperate and persecuted in Europe.

I recall the songs we used to sing in those days, prior to the formation of the State of Israel – including one about Ernest Bevin, the British Foreign Secretary, who opposed mass Jewish immigration to Palestine and was hated by the Zionist youth groups.

On 14 May 1948, the State of Israel was founded. We felt the most amazing sense of pride. After 2,000 years in exile, the Jewish people finally had a land they could call home. On that day, we all went to the central square outside the Great Synagogue in Amsterdam. The atmosphere there was incredible. People were singing and waving Israeli flags.

The establishment of the State of Israel was a turning point in Jewish history and in the life of our family. There was a collective feeling that once we had our own state, we would no longer be victims of persecution. Jehudi recalls that this made him decide to make his future in Israel. However, as a child of not yet seven, he was unable to put this into practice for some time!

For me, there was a sense of happiness; my parents were also very Zionistic and I remember this being a very positive time for the community. But, unlike Jehudi, I didn't see the establishment of Israel as having an immediate and direct impact on my future. I was 12 years old and very attached to my parents. As far as I was concerned, they had tried life in Palestine once before and had found the conditions too difficult to endure. In 1948, many young people left Holland for the newly established Jewish state, including some of my friends and their families. But the war had weakened us all considerably, so for our family Israel was simply not an option.

Sigi, Rosy, Zahava and Jehudi at the tulip fields, Keukenhof, Holland

LIFE IN AMSTERDAM
1951–1958

Looking back on the period after the war, I now realise that my main focus during those years was the well-being of my mother and father. So although they wanted me to complete the last two years of my schooling, the family's circumstances meant that I decided to leave school early – in 1951. This was something I did willingly because my natural inclination was to help my parents.

So my formal school education came to an end at the age of 16. Thanks to Nazi intervention, I had received a total of six years of formal schooling. This comprised five years after the war and one somewhat interrupted year prior to our deportation.

When I look at the New Year greetings card that I wrote to my parents when we were in Westerbork, I am still quite amazed that I was able to write and spell. Looking back, I realise how little time during my childhood was spent in school and how few opportunities there were for me to learn anything, or to do all the things that would be taken for granted in a normal childhood.

Jehudi's experiences were very different from mine. Although his early childhood must have been deeply traumatic and unsettled, he fortunately has no recollection of that time. Since he was five years old when we returned to Holland, he was able to receive an uninterrupted education in Amsterdam.

From an early age, Jehudi had very definite ideas; he wanted to live in Israel and originally wanted to study medicine. We were both active in the Zionist movement *Bnei Akiva* and that probably influenced both of us. But I think that at the time our parents had different expectations of us. I was the daughter and was expected to stay at home. I also felt very bound up with my parents' welfare. I think that Jehudi was quite independent from an early stage. When he discovered that there were 'too many doctors in Israel', he decided to change his plan and study languages in Geneva. He thought this would be more useful, although it is not clear at this stage whether he had anticipated precisely what career would result from this choice.

During my teenage years, my maternal grandmother became very ill and my mother spent long periods of time in Zürich looking after her. My father was also in poor health, having been greatly weakened by his experiences in Bergen-Belsen. He suffered from a combination of different conditions, including thyroid problems and heart disease, and needed ongoing medical treatment.

When my parents were well enough, they would take every opportunity to make the most of family life with us. We enjoyed outings together, as can be seen from the photographs shown in this chapter.

My decision to leave school was motivated by the need to help my father. I wanted to get a job to help supplement the family income. My mother's long absences from home meant that I was needed to help care for my father. I enrolled in evening classes in shorthand and

Vonderpark, June 1953

typing. I also took an English correspondence course, although at the time I didn't anticipate how useful English would be in the future!

In the mid 1950s, my father started to work independently. He had seen rainwear capes in Switzerland and was sure that the idea would be a success in Holland. Since the bicycle was the main mode of transport in the Netherlands at that time, waterproof ponchos seemed a wonderful market to explore.

My father's idea was an excellent one, but he was physically weak and in need of assistance. In 1957, he imported some sample capes to Holland and then began manufacturing them himself from home. I was also working every evening to help finish them. The capes were then sold throughout Holland.

In 1955, our family had moved to a more spacious flat in the centre of Amsterdam. It was on the first floor of a traditional Dutch canal house – our address was Amstelkade 168. This remained the

Rosy, Jehudi and Sigi outside our apartment in Amstelkade

family house until shortly before my mother emigrated to Israel in 1991.

After I left school in 1951, I started to work for a large international firm called Julius Hollander. Their headquarters were in South America and they specialised in the import and sale of hides and skins. In the beginning, I worked on telexes, but then moved on to doing typing. My boss was Benno Hess and I really enjoyed working for him. I remember the glowing personal reference that he wrote for me when I left the firm for my next job.

Having worked for Julius Hollander for over two years, I was ready for a new challenge and so, through people that I knew, I was able to obtain work at the Jewish Community Centre, the central Jewish welfare organisation in Amsterdam. Every member of the community had to pay a percentage of their income to this organisation. The Centre dealt with a wide range of needs, including care of the underprivileged and the elderly. Working for the financial director of the Jewish Community Centre meant that I had access to a lot of confidential information about the finances of many individuals. I was very pleased to be put in this responsible position.

I used to work at the office on Sunday mornings, although most of the other departments were closed over the weekend. One Sunday in 1956, there was a sudden influx of Jews from Hungary. The revolution had just taken place and consequently around 20,000 Jews, mainly Holocaust survivors, fled from Hungary at that time. A large number of these refugees fled to Holland. In the upheaval, they had left their homes in fear for their lives and arrived in Amsterdam with nothing.

The Hungarians were in urgent need of help, especially with food and housing. When they arrived at the Centre, they were told that the welfare office was closed on Sundays and that they should come back during the week. On hearing this response, I was absolutely furious and went to complain. It seemed totally unbelievable to me, in the light of our recent experiences, that Jews could treat their fellow Jews in this way.

Although this was not within the remit of my department, I was deeply upset by the indifference of some members of the community towards these refugees. After I complained, their needs were dealt with and they were eventually provided with homes and clothing.

I had been working in Amsterdam for several years when my parents began to voice mild concerns about my marital prospects. By then I was 24; there were few young men around; many had been lost and most of the survivors had chosen to go and live in Israel. Those left in Amsterdam were either younger than me or simply inappropriate.

Zahava in St Moritz, 1958

A NEW LIFE IN LONDON

By 1958, the family was very settled in Amsterdam and Jehudi was in the process of finishing his high school education. My mother decided to address the issue of my uneventful social life!

I took the first of a series of winter holidays in St Moritz with my mother. It was there that I met a group of young people from London, who became my friends. I decided that it might be a good idea to try to move to London, since I knew a lot of people there and I was ready for a change of scene.

With the help of contacts, my friends wrote to Rabbi Dr Solomon Schonfeld to ask for his help in finding me a job that would enable me to go and settle in London. Dr Schonfeld was a young and charismatic rabbi. Before the war, he had been instrumental in organising the safe passage of thousands of orphaned Jewish children from Eastern Europe to England, and finding them places in Jewish homes. Despite the personal risks, he had continued his work during the war. After the war was over, he was active in organising the transfer to England of orphaned survivors, who had returned to their homes in Eastern Europe and had to face vicious antisemitism and persecution. The orphans who had arrived in England were obviously in need of many things, among which education was a priority. To this end, Dr Schonfeld became the founder of the Jewish Schools Movement in London.

It was Dr Schonfeld's offer of employment that finally led to my decision to move to London. For a short time, I was employed as Dr Schonfeld's secretary. After a while, he suggested that I take up teaching – he was desperately short of teaching staff in his schools. Since I had no teaching qualifications and limited experience of education, I was reluctant to take up this well-intentioned offer. I did not feel that it would be fair on the children. In the end, it was agreed that I would work at a nursery school. This suited me very well as I had always loved young children. I worked first at the Hasmonean School in Edgware and then at Menorah Primary School in Golders Green from 1958 to 1962.

Zahava at Hasmonean Nursery School with one of her young pupils, summer 1960

The Orthodox community in Golders Green really took me under their wing and were wonderful to me in every way. I used to go to the Golders Green Beth Hamedrash Synagogue or *Munks*, as it was known, a community of German Jews. I was the recipient of a great deal of hospitality and I used to go for *Shabbat* meals to different families. The Kruskal family, in particular, who were also Dutch and had been exchange prisoners in Bergen-Belsen, treated me like a daughter.

During the school holidays, I used to return to Holland to join my family for short breaks by the sea. This photo shows us taking the sea air in Scheveningen in 1961.

Rosy, Sigi, Zahava and Jehudi enjoying the sea air in Scheveningen, 1961

This pattern of life – work in London and short breaks in Holland – continued until my 27th birthday, 5 August 1962, when I was in Holland visiting my family. My father had been ill, but was recovering. The next day, I was going to an educational seminar in

Montreux, Switzerland. I had my flight tickets and was looking forward to going.

My admiration and respect for my father were immense and, in general, I always did what he asked of me. So when he asked me if – as a favour to him – I would meet a young man who was the son of some mutual acquaintances, I agreed, mainly to please my father as my mind was on other things at the time.

So I went with my mother to the kosher restaurant in Scheveningen and Ralph Kohn was there with his parents. He was a 35-year-old pharmacologist. His family was also of Eastern European origin although born in Germany. After leaving Leipzig in 1933, they went to live in Amsterdam. They were acquaintances of my parents, but they did not know each other very well. Ralph's parents were on holiday in Scheveningen. Like me, Ralph was living in London and was visiting his parents. We had a perfectly pleasant conversation and I thought very little about it at the time. I also met up with another old school friend and the three of us spent some time talking. I think Ralph did ask if there was any possibility I might put off my trip to Montreux in order to spend time with him, but since I had planned to go to the seminar, I had no intention of cancelling it.

On the day that I returned to London, I received a message at work that Ralph had called. Clearly, this was a rather determined young man! From that time onwards, things moved very swiftly. We went out with each other from September to December 1962, after which we became engaged. My parents, who thought that in the past I'd perhaps been a bit hesitant about other prospective fiancés, now expressed concerns that I might be acting somewhat precipitously!

Fortuitously, my parents were members of the same *shtiebel* as Ralph's. There was a great sense that our union was meant to be. It was also very reassuring for both sets of parents that they were known to each other and had mutual friends.

We were married on 12 March 1963 at the Jacob Obrecht Synagogue, Amsterdam, and a whole new chapter of my life was to begin.

Zahava and Ralph, civil wedding, 25 February 1963

Zahava and Ralph on their wedding day, 12 March 1963

Rosy and Sigi, Amsterdam, 1960

Rosy with Jehudi and Zahava, January 1963

Ralph and Zahava with their first daughter, Hephzibah, April 1964

Zahava holding Hephzi and her second daughter, Michelle, December 1965

Three generations: Rosy and Sigi, Zahava, Hephzi and Michelle, 1965

Rosy and Sigi, with granddaughter Michelle, December 1966

Rosy and Sigi with granddaughters Hephzi and Michelle, June 1967

Michelle (left) and Hephzi, with their baby sister Maxine, 1973

Zahava and Ralph at home with their three daughters: Michelle, Hephzi and Maxine, 1978

Hephzi's wedding, with sisters Michelle (left) and Maxine, 14 March 1993

Family group at the wedding of Hephzi and Steven Rudofsky, 14 March 1993

Hephzi with her grandmother, Rosy, 14 March 1993

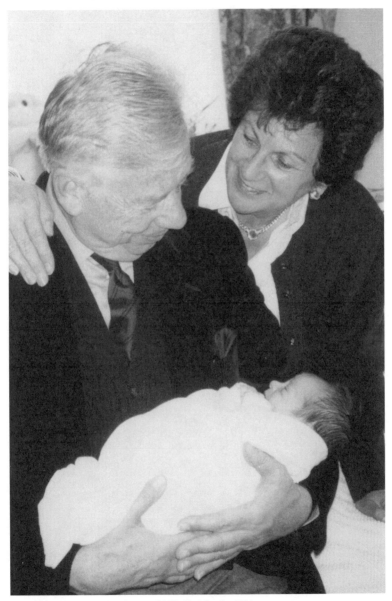

Ralph and Zahava with their first grandchild, Alex, October 1994

Four generations: Hephzi and Alex, Zahava and Rosy, Israel, April 1995

Family holiday in Florida for Ralph's 75th birthday, December 2002

Wedding of Michelle and Michael da Costa, with Ralph and Zahava, 30 November 2003

Family group at Alex's Barmitzvah, November 2007

Zahava with her grandson, Alex, November 2007

Zahava with her grandson, Theo da Costa, 2007

Zahava with her granddaughter, Talia, September 2007

Three grandchildren, Talia and Alex Rudofsky and Theo Da Costa, September 2008

Grandchildren Alex and Talia Rudofsky, Theo da Costa and Sam Judge, September 2013

Family photo at Zahava and Ralph's 50th wedding anniversary celebration, 10 March 2013

Zahava, July 2006

REFLECTIONS SIXTY YEARS ON

Looking back at my childhood, our suffering in Bergen-Belsen and our separation from Jehudi, it is truly miraculous that each member of my immediate family emerged after the war. I am profoundly grateful for the fact that we were reunited, that we became a close unit and enjoyed a rich family life together. Our story is an incredible one and I feel that my parents would very much have wanted it to be told.

Against all the odds – and unlike so many millions – Jehudi and I both survived and were able to live rewarding lives and create families of our own. It is difficult to look back now, over 60 years since the end of the war, and assess accurately the impact that my experiences in the war years – and specifically in the concentration camps – had on my later life. Piecing together the story of my past has raised many questions. Undoubtedly, my experiences influenced the choices that I made and the life that I led; yet there are few easy answers. My involvement and participation in this project has been a remarkable and often overwhelming journey.

The seeds for this book were sown many years ago during conversations with our children, especially our eldest daughter, Hephzibah, who wanted to hear my story. The family felt it was crucial that this chapter in history be chronicled for our children and for posterity. Throughout my adult life, I have been reticent about lifting the lid on my early years, yet there was a sense that if the story was not told now, perhaps it might never surface.

No matter how often I go back over the sequence of events, I still marvel at the many twists of fate that led to our survival: the last-minute decision to remove us from the Auschwitz transport; the perverse and arbitrary nature of the SS's decision not to send Jehudi to a concentration camp with the other babies from the orphanage because he looked like an 'Aryan child'; the fact that no one ever betrayed him when he was in hiding. Ultimately, when we were so precariously close to the end, our early release from Bergen-Belsen at the end of January 1945 saved us. But while it is possible to look at this remarkable chain of events that led to our survival, it is impossible to do so without remembering the millions for whom the pendulum swung in the opposite direction.

My parents' overriding priority after the war was to recreate a normal family life for us. Their desire to shield me, as far as possible, from everything that was bad, carried me through my time in the camps. Afterwards, we spoke little of our experiences as a family. My mother was very conscious of trying to limit the damage that had been done. She did not want to feel like a victim – and did not want us to feel that way either. Her objective in bringing us up was to prepare us for our future lives and not dwell on the horrors of the past.

In my adult life, I never wanted anyone's sympathy, nor to draw attention to myself by talking about experiences that I had consciously put behind me. When asked about my experiences directly, I was reluctant to speak about them – not least because I was not sure if my recollections were accurate.

People often seem surprised that I appear to be so 'normal' when my childhood was so out of the ordinary. I credit this to the incredible strength of character of my parents, who provided me with love, security and a very strong sense of worth. I think it is impossible to overestimate the importance for a young child of growing up in a secure, strong family unit. I was also fortunate to have had a happy childhood before the war and, despite everything that I saw and suffered in the camps, my mother was able to stay with me. Few complete families survived the camps, and the miracle of us emerging as a complete family was a huge factor in my emotional survival.

Of course, my parents' desire for us to grow up unencumbered by the heavy burden of the Holocaust could never be entirely possible. Nobody could experience such trauma and emerge unscathed. But now, 60 years later with memories somewhat faded, it is hard to assess precisely how the experiences affected me. Certainly, I was deeply troubled by the fact that my parents suffered ill health for so long after the war. My father never fully recovered – a continual reminder of the legacy of the camps.

My mother had always put the family first in all aspects of her life, and in many ways, my life followed her example. Consequently, I gave up school to help my family, both financially and domestically. It was something I felt I should do and the decision was taken willingly. In general, I definitely felt very protective towards my parents and this was probably intensified because I had witnessed their suffering in the camps. I always saw myself primarily in a supporting role – first as a daughter, and later on as a wife and mother. The needs of the family were of paramount importance.

My parents' greatest wish was that we should create new and individual lives for ourselves, and I think that to a large extent their hopes have been realised. Meeting my husband Ralph and having three daughters focussed my mind on so much that was new and positive. In fact, I was so fulfilled in that role that I didn't even stop and look back for many years.

Jehudi found his future in Israel which, as we know, was created largely as a result of the destruction of European Jewry. Although he has no recollection of his early years, Jehudi does remember feeling that he was part of a tolerated minority in Holland. Leaving Europe to make a new life in Israel – a land of our own, where we could be free from fear of persecutions – was the logical choice for him. To this day, I am still amazed that my little brother, who spent his early life in hiding in an orphanage and in the care of a Protestant family, emerged with such a strong sense of his Jewish identity.

In his adult life, Jehudi has enjoyed a successful career as a diplomat, representing Israel in both Europe and North America. From 1983-88, he was the minister responsible for cultural affairs at the Israeli embassy in Bonn. He was promoting Jewish culture at the very heart of Germany, where 50 years earlier the process to destroy European Jewry had begun. After that, from 2003-2007 Jehudi was the Israeli Ambassador to Belgium and Luxembourg.

Looking back at that time, we are living proof that despite their best efforts, the Nazis did not succeed in wiping us out. I feel blessed that I was able to live a complete, happy and fulfilling life, surrounded by a loving husband, three devoted daughters and three grandchildren (so far), all of whom have brought me a deep sense of joy and purpose.

In piecing together these fragments of my early life, I have relived many of the horrific events which I experienced and witnessed in my childhood. Today, as I finish telling my story, my greatest wish is that such atrocities should never happen again. My hope is that with kindness, compassion and tolerance, we can all work together to prevent a repeat of the Nazi nightmare.

Zahava Kohn and Hephzibah Rudofsky at Redbridge Interschool Seminar, hosted by King Solomon High School to mark Holocaust Memorial Day, 24th January 2013

AFTERWORD

The publication of *Fragments of a Lost Childhood* in 2009 marked the opening of a new chapter in my life. When it first appeared, I shared the book with a number of friends from far and wide. Many could not quite comprehend my family's experiences in the war years and were unable to reconcile the woman they had known for so long with her tragic history. I was deeply moved by their thoughts and comments. My eldest daughter, Hephzibah, encouraged me to speak about my experiences publicly and organised a programme to tell my story to a wider audience, specifically to young adults in schools (www. survivingtheholocaust.co.uk).

As I watched my grandchildren grow up I became acutely aware of the importance to their generation of hearing accounts from those dark days at first hand, while some of my generation are still alive to tell the 'tale'.

We started the programme in early 2010. Since then I have addressed many groups of schoolchildren in the UK to tell them my 'story' and answer their questions. The response has been astonishing.

I must confess that I initially found it a very daunting experience as I am not particularly at ease being the focus of this attention. Furthermore, this is not a topic I find easy to speak about. In fact, until the book was published, I rarely referred to our wartime experiences, even when asked to do so. However, slowly I began to share my family's story with others.

During our school visits, I have been very impressed by the young adults we have met. They come from all walks of life: all backgrounds, religions and cultures, yet their questions are invariably sensitive, searching and intelligent. This fills me with great hope for the future. I feel very fortunate to have had this opportunity to share my story and would like to thank the teachers and pupils who have been so welcoming and engaging over the past few years. But in particular, I would like to thank my family for their unstinting support and, in particular, my daughter Hephzibah for all she has done to enable this programme to be presented to so many young people in schools throughout the country.

In March 2013, my husband Ralph and I celebrated our 50th wedding anniversary with family and friends. I feel supremely blessed to be surrounded by my loving family and in the fact that I am able to continue to live a full and enriching life.

October 2013